STEPHENSONS' BRITAIN

STEPHENSONS' BRITAIN
Derrick Beckett

Line Illustrations by Malcolm Kaye

DAVID & CHARLES
Newton Abbot   London   North Pomfret (Vt)

British Library Cataloguing in Publication Date

Beckett, Derrick
   Stephensons' Britain.
   1. Stephenson, George, *1781–1848*
   2. Stephenson, Robert
   3. Civil Engineering
   I.Title
   624   TA140.S/

ISBN 0–7153–8269–1

Typeset by ABM Typographics Limited, Hull
and printed in Great Britain by
Biddles Ltd, Guildford, Surrey
for David & Charles (Publishers) Limited
Brunel House   Newton Abbot   Devon

Published in the United States of America
by David & Charles Inc
North Pomfret   Vermont 05053   USA

PREFACE

On Tuesday 9 June 1981, I attended the George Stephenson Bicentenary Lecture held at the headquarters of the Institution of Mechanical Engineers, Birdcage Walk, Westminster. George Stephenson was elected the first president of the institution in 1847 and the capacity audience was addressed by J. T. van Riemsdijk, Keeper of Mechanical and Civil Engineering, The Science Museum, who chose as his theme 'The Hero as Engineer'. The engineer has not popularly been associated with the qualities of a hero but van Riemsdijk correctly observed that the qualities of a number of engineers who pioneered the development of the mechanical and civil engineering aspects of railways are essentially the qualities of a hero. Arguably, George Stephenson can be considered as the most heroic figure in the development of railways and certainly the most courageous. L. T. C. Rolt in his biography on George and Robert Stephenson makes the sweeping statement: 'George Stephenson is the most famous engineer who ever lived'. Yet paradoxically, a short while after the lecture, I asked one of the locals in a village just over a mile from George Stephenson's birthplace in Wylam for directions to the cottage in which he was born — the reply was, 'Never heard of it'.

It is hoped that this book will demonstrate the heroic qualities of George Stephenson and his son Robert and, as with *Brunel's Britain,* the greater emphasis will be on the works of Robert Stephenson and his contribution to the civil engineering aspects of railways.

The lives of the Stephensons and the Brunels ran in parallel, embracing a mere ninety years:

MARC ISAMBARD BRUNEL	25 April 1769 – 12 December 1849
GEORGE STEPHENSON	9 June 1781 – 12 August 1848
ISAMBARD KINGDOM BRUNEL	9 April 1806 – 15 September 1859
ROBERT STEPHENSON	16 October 1803 – 12 October 1859

It is a remarkable coincidence that father and son, Stephenson and Brunel, of widely differing personalities, education and talents, should jointly make such an immense contribution to the development of civil

5

and mechanical engineering in a similar time-scale. Comparisons between the Stephensons and the Brunels are inevitable, but the aim of this book is not to argue that the talents of the Stephensons were superior to the Brunels or otherwise — in fact they complement each other. Its primary aim, as with *Brunel's Britain,* is to chronicle their engineering works as they exist today and to encourage the reader to inspect and appreciate the architectural and technical quality of their work. To facilitate this, a gazetteer is included and London is used as the base from which to commence a tour of the numerous locations.

CONTENTS

	Introduction	9
	Chronicle of People and Events	23
1	George Stephenson	27
2	Robert Stephenson	63
3	London & Birmingham Railway	77
4	Chester & Holyhead Railway	108
5	Collapse of the Bridge Over the River Dee	120
6	Britannia and Conwy Tubular Bridges	131
7	Bridging the Tyne and Tweed	153
8	Work Overseas	175
9	The Stephensons and the Brunels	184
10	The Stephensons' Legacy	194
	Gazetteer	199
	Technical Appendices	215
	I Structural mechanics	215
	II The Dee Bridge	216
	III The Britannia and Conwy Tubular Bridges	218
	IV High Level Bridge, Newcastle	227
	Bibliography	229
	Acknowledgements	233
	Index	235

"Mr Stephenson, what do you consider to be the most powerful force in nature?" "Oh!" said he, in a gallant spirit, "I will soon answer that question: it is the eye of a woman for the man who loves her; for if a woman look with affection on a young man, and he should go to the uttermost ends of the earth, the recollection of that look will bring him back: there is no other force in nature could do that."

(SAMUEL SMILES, *Lives of the Engineers*, Vol 3)

INTRODUCTION

*. . . it is light bottled up in the earth for tens of thousands of years —
light, absorbed by plants and vegetables, being necessary for the condensation of carbon during the process of their growth, if it be not carbon in another form — and now, after being buried in the earth for long
ages in fields of coal, that latent light is again brought forth and liber-
ated, made to work as in that locomotive, for great human purposes . . .*
(George Stephenson on coal, SAMUEL SMILES,
Lives of the Engineers, Vol 3)

In the year 1810, a group of owners or lessees of coalfields in Northumberland and Durham, known as the 'Grand Allies', sank a pit at the village of Killingworth a few miles to the north of Newcastle. A pumping
engine of the Newcomen type, modified by Smeaton, was installed to
clear water from the pit, but it was ineffective for about a year. One
Saturday afternoon George Stephenson, employed as a brakesman at
the nearby West Moor Pit, inspected the engine and declared that in a
week's time he could send workmen to the bottom. The following Friday afternoon the workmen were sent to the bottom. This event demonstrated Stephenson's potential as a mechanical engineer and his
talents were soon recognised. Within fifteen years he had made an immense contribution to the use of steam for locomotion and with the
opening of the Liverpool & Manchester Railway in 1830, established
the steam railway as a revolutionary and viable means of transportation.
Coal and steam are, of course, central features of George Stephenson's
life and in order to put his work in perspective, it is necessary to survey
the development of coal mining and the use of steam up to the end of the
first decade of the nineteenth century. In the three decades which followed, the further progress of the steam locomotive can largely be attributed to George and Robert Stephenson, and the locomotive works,
Robert Stephenson & Co, established at Forth Street, Newcastle, in
1823 was soon to gain an international reputation.

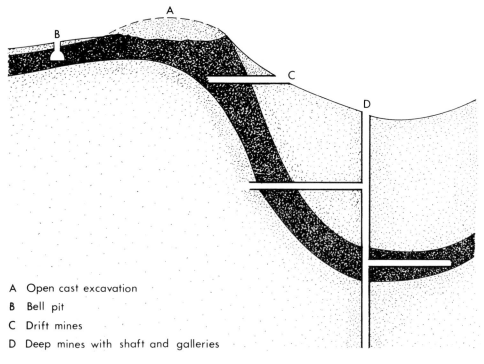

A Open cast excavation
B Bell pit
C Drift mines
D Deep mines with shaft and galleries

Fig 1 Methods of access to coal seams

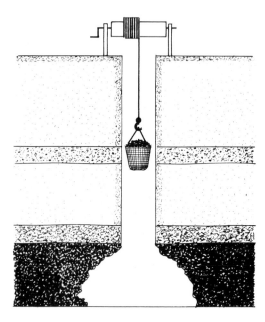

Fig 2 Extraction of coal from a bell pit with a hand winch and basket

Coal Mining

Coal is a rock formed by the accumulation of vegetable matter which has been subjected to pressure and Britain's coal seams were formed in the Carboniferous period 270 to 350 million years ago. The seams of Northumberland and Durham occur mainly in the upper strata of the carboniferous rocks and stretch at the widest point about 20 miles (32km) inland from the coast. Coal has been associated with the region since Roman times and coal working commenced about 700 years ago. The first access to coal was at outcrops where the coal was picked from the surface (Fig 1). Coal was also worked from shallow drifts and bell pits. Bell pits were rarely more than 25ft (7.6m) deep and a simple hand winch was used to wind the coal up in baskets (Fig 2). Coal was cut away round the pit bottom until danger of collapse forced it to be abandoned.

Coal working expanded slowly until the sixteenth century, but thereafter demand rapidly increased as our forests became depleted and efforts were made to replace wood by coal in metallurgy. Deeper shafts were sunk, up to 400ft (122m), and this brought about the problem of drainage as the shafts extended below the water table and water accumulated at lower levels. This was aggravated by the need to provide adequate ventilation and by the presence of explosive and suffocating gases, methane and carbon dioxide. These problems were gradually overcome with the use of steam engines for pumping and the development of the safety lamp (see page 33).

The coal was worked by cutting headings into the coal seams and dividing the seams up into large pillars by roads driven at right angles. The pillars were then removed and the roof supported by timber props. This technique, known as bord and pillar working (bord is a Saxon word for road), was used by miners in Northumberland and Durham until well after the nationalisation of the coal industry in 1947. At a depth of about 900ft (274m), there is a risk of the pillars or props being crushed owing to the weight of overlying strata. Other methods of extraction were therefore developed, in particular, the long wall system, c1850.

The hand winch was no longer adequate to raise the coal to the surface and was replaced by the horse whim or gin (Fig 3). The horizontal rope drum rotates on a vertical axis, the horse being attached to the end of a horizontal beam. The coal was raised to the surface in small baskets known as corves. The horse whim was gradually replaced by steam winding engines and the hemp ropes were replaced by wire ropes between 1830 and 1840.

Plate 1 A hand drill in the preserved coal workings at the North of England Open Air Museum, Beamish. Loose gunpowder would be poured into the hole and tamped with clay (*Frances Gibson-Smith*)

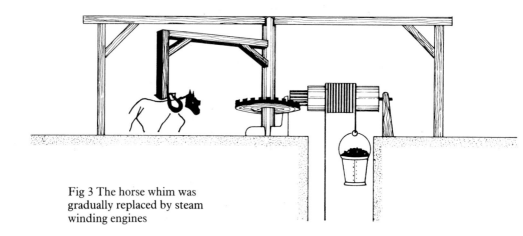

Fig 3 The horse whim was gradually replaced by steam winding engines

The rapid expansion of coal mining in Northumberland and Durham in the sixteenth century was facilitated by the growth of the sea trade from the Tyne to London. Although coal was worked from pits sunk in the proximity of the Tyne, its transportation from the pit head to the riverside was the source of considerable mechanical ingenuity which led to the evolution in the North East of the railway and the locomotive and their subsequent development to form a nationwide transportation system. Initially, coal was carried to the river in panniers on horses' backs and subsequently in horse-drawn carts. It has been recorded that in about 1630, wagons with wooden flanged wheels running along wooden tracks were in use. Subsequently, strips of iron were attached to the top of the wooden rails to prevent wear, and later various shapes of iron rail were designed to replace wooden rails. The Wylam wagon-way, which passed the cottage in which George Stephenson was born, used wooden rails until 1807. On reaching the river, the wagons were unloaded at wooden landing stages, known as staiths. Self-acting inclines were also used to transport coal to the staiths — the descending full wagons drawing the empty wagons up the incline. It was not until 1812 that steam locomotives were used on colliery railways.

Steam

As mentioned already, one of the major problems to be overcome in the extraction of coal from deep mines was pumping out water which flooded the headings. In 1698 Thomas Savery (1650–1715), a military engineer, obtained a patent for 'Raiseing of Water . . . by the Impellant Force of Fire' and in 1702 published *The Miner's Friend* which described a steam pump. It is doubtful whether the pump was used in a mine but his patent, which extended to 1733, covered any method of raising water by fire. The first practical and reliable steam engines were built by Thomas Newcomen (1663–1729), an ironmonger from Dartmouth. As a result of Savery's patent, which was acquired by a group of speculators, including Newcomen, heavy royalty payments were demanded, but after the patent expired in 1733 its use spread rapidly and it has been estimated that by 1765 at least one hundred Newcomen-type atmospheric 'fire engines' were in use in the Tyneside coalfields.

The components of Newcomen's engine as constructed in 1712 are shown in Fig 4. The boiler produces steam at atmospheric pressure which passes into an open-topped vertical cylinder containing a piston

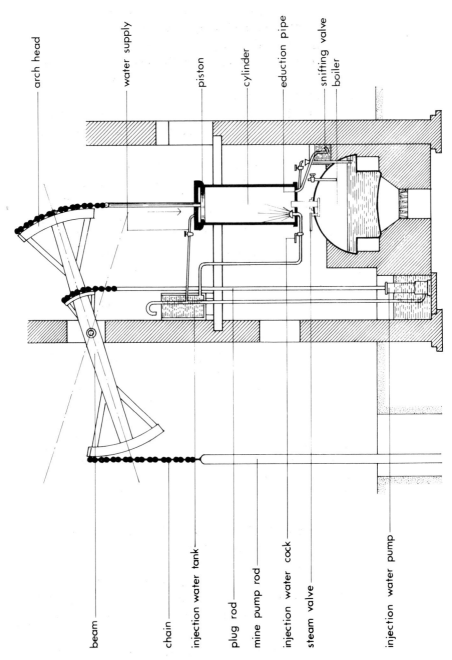

arch head

water supply

piston

cylinder

eduction pipe

sniffing valve

boiler

beam

chain

injection water tank

plug rod

mine pump rod

injection water cock

steam valve

injection water pump

Fig 4 The components of the atmospheric pumping engine as constructed by Thomas Newcomen in 1712

which is connected via a piston rod to a chain attached to the arched head of a rocking beam. The leather piston ring was kept pressed against the cylinder wall by means of a layer of water above. As the steam entered the cylinder, it discharged any water or air present through an eduction pipe and the piston rose to the top. The connection to the boiler was closed and this was followed by partial condensation of the steam by a jet of water. The resulting partial vacuum allowed the atmospheric pressure to push the piston down and raise the pump rods. The cycle was then repeated by the admission of more steam on opening the steam valve.

John Smeaton (1724–92), the earliest of the great British civil engineers, carried out a number of observations on Newcomen engines in the Newcastle district and improved their thermal efficiency from 0.5 to 1.4 per cent in 1774. However, Smeaton's work was overshadowed by the perception of James Watt (1736–1819), an instrument maker at Glasgow University. He was working on the repair of a model of a Newcomen engine in about 1763 and realised that high thermal losses occurred during the raising and lowering of the temperature of the cylinder at each stroke, that is, when the steam was admitted and condensed by a jet of cold water. Subsequently he wrote:

I perceived that in order to make the best use of steam, it was necessary — first, that the cylinder should be maintained always as hot as the steam which entered it; and, secondly, that when the steam was condensed, the water of which it was composed, and the injection itself should be cooled down to 100° (F), or lower, where that was possible. The means of accomplishing these points did not immediately present themselves; but early in 1765 it occurred to me, that if a communication were opened between a cylinder containing steam, and another vessel which was exhausted of air and fluids, the steam, as an elastic fluid, would immediately rush into the empty vessel, and continue so to do until it has established an equilibrium, and if that vessel were kept very cool by an injection, or otherwise, more steam would continue to enter until the whole was condensed . . .

Thus the separate condenser evolved and the principle is illustrated in Fig 5. Watt insulated the cylinder by means of a steam jacket and patented his separate condenser in 1769. In 1773 Watt entered into partnership with a Birmingham industrialist, Matthew Boulton (1728–1809), and by 1792 the Boulton and Watt engine achieved a thermal efficiency of 4.5 per cent, three times that of the Newcomen engines. A contributory factor to this improved efficiency was that they were able to take advantage of the patent (1774) of John Wilkinson (1728–1808) for a boring mill, which meant that large diameter bores could be cut

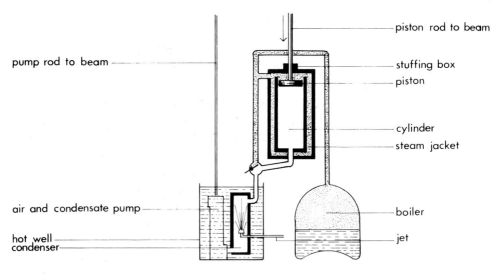

Fig 5 In 1765 James Watt perceived that the efficiency of the atmospheric engine could be increased by introducing a separate condenser

very accurately. The Boulton and Watt engines were used extensively in various industries with the exception of the coal industry.

The Newcomen engine was well established and fuel costs were not a significant factor. In 1800 there were only six Boulton and Watt engines in use in the Northumberland and Durham coalfield. As we have seen, George Stephenson's first opportunity to demonstrate his mechanical engineering talents, in 1811, was with the repair of a faulty Smeaton-designed atmospheric engine of the Newcomen type.

The atmospheric engines working at pressures of 5-10psi (0.035-0.07N/mm²) were far too heavy for practical application to locomotion. In 1784 William Murdock (1754–1839), one of James Watt's assistants, constructed a three-wheeled toy steam engine which worked at high pressure and was provided with valves for regulating the passage of steam. The copper boiler was heated with a spirit lamp and the piston had a stroke of 2in (51mm) and was ¾in (19mm) in diameter. Although it worked successfully — on one occasion it fairly outran the speed of its inventor (Smiles) — Murdock did not progress the design. He was later to make an important contribution to the use of gas lighting.

In 1796, Richard Trevithick (1771–1833), who was working in a Cornish tin mine, experimented with model steam engines and in 1801 built a full-size road locomotive, the first in Britain. The vertical cylinder was partly sunk into the cylindrical internally fired boiler and the piston rod drove the rear wheels by a cross head with slide bars and connecting

16

rod. The exhaust steam was turned up the chimney to increase the draught. It had a loaded weight of about 1½ tons. In 1803, Trevithick built another steam carriage which was demonstrated in London but there was little public interest. A year later, he built a steam locomotive, which weighed about 5 tons without water and ran on the 9¾ mile (15.7 km) L-section cast-iron plate tramway from Penydarren iron-works to the Glamorganshire canal. The locomotive had smooth flange-less wheels and thus Trevithick established that smooth wheels would provide sufficient adhesion to transmit the tractive force. It was also significant that there was extensive breakage of the cast-iron tramway plates and thus the wooden or iron tracks built for horse haulage could not sustain the loads imposed by early locomotives.

In 1805, a similar engine was built by one of Trevithick's mechanics for the Gateshead ironworks, Tyne, of Hawkes and Crawshay. It was possibly the first railway locomotive with flanged wheels and ran on wooden rails. It was ordered by Christopher Blackett, owner of the Wylam colliery, to run on the wagonway. Apparently, the locomotive did not leave the works and was converted into a stationary engine. Trevithick visited Newcastle several times between 1805 and 1808 and was known to George Stephenson. About twenty years later Robert Stephenson met Richard Trevithick in entirely different circumstances at the port of Cartagena, Colombia, on his return from South America (see Chapter 8).

Trevithick made a final attempt to demonstrate the potential of the locomotive and a new engine *Catch me who can* (Plate 2) was built in 1808 to run on a circular track near Euston Square. The venture was not successful and between 1816 and 1827, Trevithick attempted to apply his engineering talents in South America, but returned penniless and was buried at Dartford in 1833. Trevithick's contribution to the de-velopment of the locomotive was not generally recognised and certainly not by George Stephenson.

In April 1811, John Blenkinsop (1783–1831) obtained a patent for a rack locomotive (Plate 3) which employed two vertical cylinders driving separate cranks geared to a rack wheel which meshed with a rack cast on the edge rails on one side of the track. It was built by Matthew Murray (1765–1826) who was the first engineer to employ two cylinders which worked alternately from the same axle.

The Blenkinsop/Murray engines were employed on the 3½ mile (5.6 km) railway from the Middleton collieries to Leeds from August 1812. The use of a rack drive demonstrated lack of conviction of the

Plate 2 A conjectural model of Richard Trevithick's locomotive *Catch-me-who-can*, built in 1808 to run on a circular track near Euston Square (*Science Museum, London*)

Plate 3 A Science Museum drawing of John Blenkinsop's rack locomotive patented in 1811. The rack was cast on edge rails on one side of the track; the engine had an inside wooden frame and weighed about 5 tons (*Science Museum, London*)

ability to obtain adequate adhesion with smooth wheel contact. In 1812, Christopher Blackett ordered a second locomotive to run on the Wylam wagonway which had been modified in 1808, the wooden rails being replaced by cast-iron plate rails. It was a combination of Trevithick's and Blenkinsop's designs and was a failure.

A third engine, again employing the rack rail, proved to be more successful, but the rail design was inadequate to sustain the weight of about 6 tons (60kN). Between 1813 and 1814, William Hedley (1779–1843), the viewer of Wylam colliery, carried out some experiments to determine the adhesion of smooth wheels to smooth rails and developed a four-wheeled locomotive, the *Wylam Dilly*, to run on the Wylam plateway. Again, it was too heavy for the track and it was subsequently converted into an eight-wheeled locomotive (Plate 4). The two vertical cylinders were mounted on each side of a wrought-iron boiler and drove a single crank shaft coupled to the wheels by spur gearing. The steam pressure was 50 psi (3.51 kg/sq cm) and the total weight 8³/₁₀ tons (83kN).

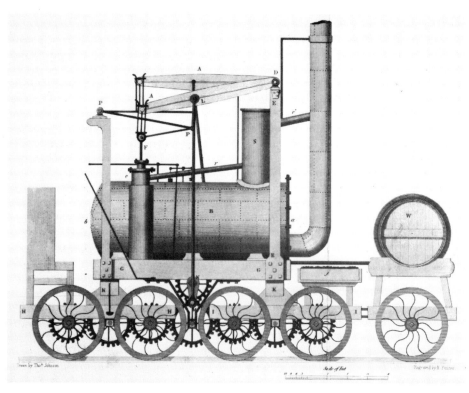

Plate 4 William Hedley's original four-wheeled locomotive was converted to an eight-wheeled locomotive to reduce the load on the track. From an engraving in Ward's *A Practical Treatise on Railroads*, 1825 *(Science Museum, London)*

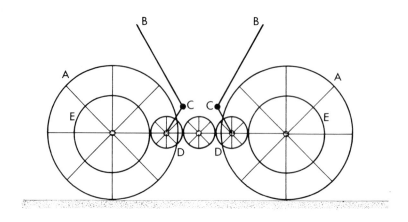

Fig 6 George Stephenson's first locomotive was designed with a spur wheel arrangement to replace Blenkinsop's cogged rail

20

It was not until 1813 that George Stephenson began working on the design of a locomotive. It was for the Killingworth colliery a few miles to the north of Newcastle and the project was sponsored by Sir Thomas Liddell (Lord Ravensworth). After ten months of trial and error, the first version was tested on 25 July 1814. The 6 ton (60kN) engine was capable of pulling a load of 30 tons (300kN) up an incline of 1 in 450 at a speed of 4mph (6kph). The construction followed in part Blenkinsop's design with two vertical cylinders set into the boiler and the steam pressure was again 50psi (3.5kg/sq cm). However, Blenkinsop's cogged rail was replaced by a spur wheel arrangement (Fig 6) which transmitted the power to four flanged wheels (A). The connecting rods (B) had cranks (C), each of which was attached to a spur wheel arrangement (D) and these 1ft (30cm) diameter wheels were geared to 2ft (61cm) diameter wheels (E) on the axles of the flanged wheels (A). The central 1ft (30cm) diameter spur wheel maintained the cranks at right

Plate 5 One of the numerous modifications to George Stephenson's first locomotive was to replace the spur-wheel arrangement by a chain system. From an original water-colour by G. F. Westcott (*Science Museum, London*)

angles to each other and governed the effect of the tractive effort (G. Drysdale Dempsey). Even Samuel Smiles referred to *Blucher*, as the locomotive was called, as 'a somewhat cumbrous and clumsy machine'. To improve its efficiency, numerous modifications included passing the waste steam up the chimney to increase the draught and replacing the spur wheel arrangement by a chain system passing over geared wheels connected to the flanged driving wheel axles. This version is illustrated in Plate 5. The chain system was subsequently abandoned and the front and rear wheels were connected by rods and cranks on the outside.

George Stephenson is popularly known as 'the father of the locomotive', a statement originating from Dr Dionysius Lardner at a lecture to the Literary and Philosophical Society of Newcastle in 1836 (L. T. C. Rolt). The son of Lord Ravensworth, the Hon H. T. Liddell, in proposing a toast to George Stephenson at a banquet in 1844, declared that he 'constructed the first locomotive that ever went by its own spontaneous movement along rails' (L. T. C. Rolt). Both these statements grossly exaggerate the facts, but a more realistic view is that by December 1830, George and Robert Stephenson had incorporated in the 2–2–0 *Planet*, built for the Liverpool & Manchester Railway, all the essential features of the 'modern' steam engine (see page 54). There has been little fundamental development since 1830.

CHRONICLE OF
PEOPLE AND EVENTS

c1200	Coal extracted from bell pits up to about 25ft (7.6m) deep
c1600	Wood famine in England and efforts made to replace wood by coal in metallurgy. Mine shafts up to about 400ft (122m) deep and severe problems with drainage
c1630	Wooden rails used to facilitate the haulage of coal wagons
1660	Royal Society founded, whose purpose was 'the general advancement of natural science'
1698	Thomas Savery (1650–1715) obtained a patent for 'Raiseing of water . . . by the impellant force of fire'
1702	Savery published the *Miner's Friend* which described a steam pump and the patent for raising water was extended until 1733
1712	Thomas Newcomen (1663–1729) erected an atmospheric steam engine at Dudley Castle in Staffordshire
1733	Savery's patent expired and the use of the Newcomen atmospheric engine spread more rapidly
c1738	Early use of cast-iron rails for wagon ways
1765	About one hundred Newcomen atmospheric engines in use in Tyneside area
25 April 1769	Marc Isambard Brunel born in Haqueville, Normandy
1769	James Watt (1736–1819) took out patent for 'A new method of lessening the consumption of steam and fuel in fire engines'
15 March 1771	Society of Civil Engineers founded by John Smeaton (1724–92) and other practising engineers who had already gained extensive experience

c1773	James Watt entered into partnership with Matthew Boulton (1728–1809)
1774	John Wilkinson (1728–1808) took out patent for an accurate means of boring cylinders
1776	Boulton and Watt erected two atmospheric engines with separate condensers at Bloomfield colliery, Staffordshire, and for John Wilkinson's blast furnaces at New Willey, Shropshire
9 June 1781	George Stephenson born at Wylam on the north bank of the River Tyne about 8 miles (13km) west of Newcastle
1784	William Murdock (1754–1839) constructed a three-wheel toy steam engine which worked at high pressure
1801	Richard Trevithick (1771–1833) built a full-size road locomotive with the steam at high pressure and the exhaust steam turned up the chimney
28 Nov 1802	George Stephenson married Frances Henderson (d1806) in Newburn church
16 Oct 1803	Robert Stephenson born
9 April 1806	Isambard Kingdom Brunel born in Portsmouth
1808	Richard Trevithick's *Catch me who can* ran on a circular track near Euston Square
1811	George Stephenson repaired a Newcomen-type atmospheric engine originally made by Smeaton and installed at Killingworth pit for pumping water
April 1811	John Blenkinsop (1783–1831) took out a patent for a rack locomotive to improve adhesion with the track
1814	William Hedley (1779–1843) constructed the *Wylam Dilly* to run on the Wylam plateway
25 July 1814	George Stephenson's *Blucher* underwent trials and pulled a 30 ton load up an incline of 1 in 450
1815	George Stephenson tested his safety lamps on 24 October and 4 November
2 Jan 1818	Inaugural meeting of the Institution of Civil Engineers founded by a group of young engineers
March 1820	George Stephenson married Elizabeth Hindmarsh (d1845)
April 1821	An Act of Parliament was obtained for the construction of the Stockton & Darlington Railway

11 July 1823	Robert Stephenson & Co commenced trading
18 June 1824	Robert Stephenson set sail from Liverpool for Colombia
27 Sept 1825	Ceremonial opening of the Stockton & Darlington Railway, the world's first practical steam railway. Initially steam used for goods traffic only
Nov 1827	Robert Stephenson returned from Colombia
17 June 1829	Robert Stephenson married Fanny Sanderson (d1842)
6 Oct 1829	Locomotive trials commenced at the Rainhill level of the Liverpool & Manchester Railway and Stephenson's *Rocket* wins
3 May 1830	The Canterbury & Whitstable Railway was formally opened, part-locomotive and part-cable traction
15 Sept 1830	Formal opening of the Liverpool & Manchester Railway, the first public railway to carry passengers and goods vehicles hauled by steam locomotives
17 July 1832	Opening of the Leicester & Swannington Railway
4 July 1837	The Grand Junction Railway opened throughout connecting Birmingham with Warrington
17 Sept 1838	The London & Birmingham Railway opened throughout
4 July 1844	Act of Parliament obtained for the construction of the Chester & Holyhead Railway
31 July 1845	Act of Parliament obtained for the construction of the Newcastle & Berwick Railway
24 April 1846	Robert Stephenson supervised the driving of the first pile for the High Level Bridge, Newcastle, using Nasmyth's steam hammer
18 Aug 1846	Act for regulating the gauge of railways received royal assent in favour of Stephenson's gauge of 4ft 8½in
20 Oct 1846	Cast-iron girder bridge over the River Dee at Chester inspected and passed for traffic
1847	Robert Stephenson elected MP for Whitby
27 Jan 1847	Foundation of the Institution of Mechanical Engineers and George Stephenson elected first president
24 May 1847	Collapse of the bridge over the River Dee at Chester
1848	George Stephenson married Ellen Gregory

1 May 1848	Conwy Tubular Bridge opened for single-line traffic
12 Aug 1848	George Stephenson died, buried at Trinity Church, Chesterfield
1849	Robert Stephenson elected Fellow of the Royal Society and President of the Institution of Mechanical Engineers
15 Aug 1849	Opening of the High Level Bridge, Newcastle
12 Dec 1849	Marc Isambard Brunel died
18 March 1850	Britannia Tubular Bridge opened for public traffic
29 Aug 1850	Opening of Royal Border Bridge, Berwick upon Tweed
1855	Robert Stephenson elected president of the Institution of Civil Engineers
Oct 1855	Opening of two tubular bridges in Egypt with the rails laid on top of the tubes
25 Dec 1858	Robert Stephenson and Isambard Kingdom Brunel dined in Cairo
15 Sept 1859	Isambard Kingdom Brunel died
12 Oct 1859	Robert Stephenson died
24 Nov 1859	The first train ran across the Victoria Tubular Bridge over the St Lawrence River, Montreal

1
GEORGE STEPHENSON

I will do something in coming time which will astonish all England.
(GEORGE STEPHENSON)

Early Life

George Stephenson, the second child of Robert Stephenson and Mabel Carr (see family tree), was born at the colliery village of Wylam, some 8 miles (13km) west of Newcastle, on 9 June 1781. The lower room on the left-hand side of the cottage shown in Plate 6 formed the Stephenson family home. Today, the land between the cottage and the River Tyne is designated as a picnic area and there are few visible signs that two hundred years ago the village of Wylam was surrounded by pumping engine houses, ash, coal dust and slag heaps. A wooden wagonway passed directly in front of the cottage and thus one of George Stephenson's first sights as a young child of the world around him would have been the horse-drawn coal wagons being dragged along the wooden tracks.

Old Robert Stephenson was employed as a fireman at the old pumping engine at Wylam colliery, but in about 1790 the coal at Wylam was worked out and the engine dismantled. The family moved a few miles north east to Dewley Burn (Fig 7) and old Robert was again employed as a fireman. George Stephenson's first employment associated with coal mining was to clear the coals of foreign matter and this was followed by driving the gins at Dewley and Black Callerton.

In 1795, George Stephenson at the age of fourteen, was appointed as an assistant to his father at Dewley at a wage of 1s a day. Families associated with coal mining had to accept the necessity of frequently moving home to 'follow the work' and the next move was to Jolly's Close, near the village of Newburn. There were a number of coal workings in this area and George Stephenson spent about two years as fireman to a small engine at Mid Hill, followed by a period of working on a pumping engine at Throckley Bridge, and his wages increased to 12s per week. The pit at Newburn was not successful and a new pit was sunk at Water

Plate 6 George Stephenson's birthplace at Wylam. A wooden wagonway passed directly in front of the cottage (*Frances Gibson-Smith*)

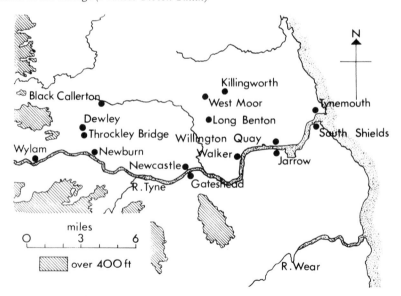

Fig 7 The Stephenson family frequently moved home in the Newcastle area to 'follow the work'

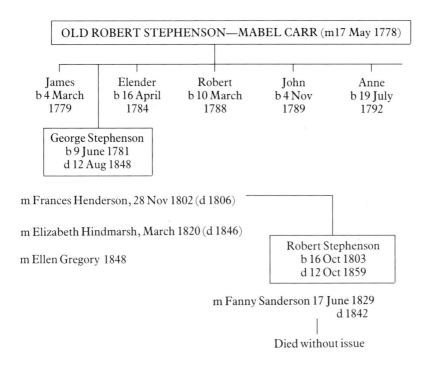

OLD ROBERT STEPHENSON—MABEL CARR (m17 May 1778)

James	Elender	Robert	John	Anne
b 4 March	b 16 April	b 10 March	b 4 Nov	b 19 July
1779	1784	1788	1789	1792

George Stephenson
b 9 June 1781
d 12 Aug 1848

m Frances Henderson, 28 Nov 1802 (d 1806)

m Elizabeth Hindmarsh, March 1820 (d 1846)

m Ellen Gregory 1848

Robert Stephenson
b 16 Oct 1803
d 12 Oct 1859

m Fanny Sanderson 17 June 1829
d 1842

Died without issue

Row about ½ mile (0.8km) west of Newburn. George was now seventeen years old and he obtained the position of engineman or plugman to the pumping engine there with his father in a position of lower status — a fireman. According to Smiles, George's duty as a plugman:

was to watch the engine to see that it kept well in work, and that the pumps were efficient in drawing the water. When the water level in the pit was lowered, and the suction became incomplete through the exposure of the suction holes, it was then his duty to proceed to the bottom of the shaft and plug the tube so that the pump should draw . . .

George Stephenson's rapid progress as a mechanic was achieved without the benefit of literacy and he was eighteen before he learnt to read (see Chapter 9).

In 1801, George moved away from the family home following further elevation of his status with an appointment as a brakesman at Dolly Pit, Black Callerton. This involved supervising the engine and machinery for movement of men and materials in and out of the pit. His wage advanced to £1 a week. George Stephenson subsequently accepted an offer to act as brakesman to a fixed engine at Willington Ballast Hill. The ballast, emptied out of the ships on their return from delivering coal to

Plate 7 George Stephenson, as portrayed by H. W. Pickersgill (*National Portrait Gallery*)

Plate 8 Newburn Church where George Stephenson and Frances Henderson were married on 28 November 1802. Stephenson had first wooed Frances' sister Anne, but she rejected his advances and he transferred his attentions to Fanny, despite her being twelve years his senior *(Frances Gibson-Smith)*

London, was drawn up in wagons to the top of the incline and then dumped. He purchased a cottage at Willington Quay, about 6 miles (9.6km) downstream from Newcastle, as a home for his first wife Fanny Henderson. They were married at Newburn church on 28 November 1802.

Robert Stephenson was born at Willington Quay on 16 October 1803. The family moved to West Moor colliery, near Killingworth in 1804. Killingworth is situated about 7 miles (11km) north of Newcastle and the colliery was one of the largest in the area. Fanny Henderson died in 1806 and George Stephenson accepted an offer to superintend a Boulton and Watt engine near Montrose in Scotland. To work on the more advanced Boulton and Watt engine must have been an attraction to Stephenson and during his absence Robert was under the care of his grandparents at Jolly's Close. On his return from Montrose,

Stephenson was to learn that his father had lost his sight as a result of an accident whilst repairing an engine. This was a depressing period in Stephenson's life (c1808) — his savings were used to buy himself out of the militia and he contemplated emigrating to America.

George persevered as a brakesman at West Moor pit, Killingworth, and in 1811, as we have seen (p9), was given the opportunity to demonstrate his talents as a mechanical engineer in repairing a pumping engine of the Newcomen type. This led to his eventual appointment as enginewright to the collieries at Killingworth. George Stephenson and his son lived in a cottage (Plate 9) on the road leading from West Moor colliery to Killingworth. In this period Stephenson erected winding and pumping engines and in 1812 laid down inclined planes to facilitate the movement of coal wagons from the pits down to the Tyne. George Stephenson's early work on locomotive design up to the design of the *Blucher* is described in the Introduction. Before continuing with Stephenson's work on track and locomotive design there was another aspect of coal mining that attracted his attention, that is, the prevention of explosions by fire-damp.

Plate 9 The Stephenson's cottage near to West Moor colliery at Killingworth (*Frances Gibson-Smith*)

The Safety Lamp

At the beginning of the nineteenth century, the best coal seams near the surface in the Newcastle area became exhausted and it was necessary to sink shafts as deep as 600ft (183m) (Singer *et al*) to reach unworked areas. Gases containing carbon monoxide, a cumulative poison, were present in shallow workings and as they became deeper an explosive mixture of methane and air (fire-damp) was encountered. Methane is a product of the conversion of decaying vegetation into coal and the gas collects in fissures in the coal and rocks. In contact with air at certain proportions (5.4 to 13.5 per cent of methane at atmospheric pressure) an explosive mixture is formed. The use of mechanical ventilation to disperse poisonous and explosive gas mixtures had only limited success. In the Killingworth area, with nearly 160 miles (257km) of coal workings, there were inevitably a number of fatalities resulting from explosions originating from the naked flame of a candle or oil lamp coming into contact with an inflammable mixture of methane and air.

In the period 1813–15 work on the development of a safety lamp was carried out almost simultaneously by W. R. Clanny (1776–1850), a medical practitioner, Sir Humphrey Davy (1778–1829), a scientist, and George Stephenson, an engine-wright.

In 1813, Clanny produced a 'blast lamp' which had a cistern of water above and below the flame, through which the surrounding air was driven by hand bellows. Although Clanny carried out further developments, his design was not accepted as it was too unwieldy.

According to Smiles, George Stephenson's theory was that if he could construct a lamp with a chimney at the top, so as to cause a strong current, it would not fire at the top of the chimney, as the burnt air would ascend with such a velocity as to prevent the inflammable air of the pit from descending towards the flame, and such a lamp, he thought, might be taken into an explosive atmosphere without risk of exploding.

Drawings were prepared in August 1815 and by 21 October the first lamp was ready for testing. Some doubt has been cast on the validity of these tests as they may not have been carried out under the most onerous conditions. However, L. T. C. Rolt in his biography of George and Robert Stephenson has produced some convincing written evidence of their validity. Sir Humphrey Davy visited the collieries near Newcastle on 24 August 1815 and, following three months of scientific investigation, he presented a paper 'On the fire-damp of coal mines and on methods of lighting the mine so as to prevent its explosion' to the Royal Society on 9 November 1815. By 30 November, Stephenson had tested his third lamp but Sir Humphrey Davy was awarded £2,000 for 'his invention of the safety lamp' (Rolt) and Stephenson a consolation prize of £100. Later, the balance was partially redressed when a group of Stephenson's supporters raised a further £1,000 through public subscription.

Locomotive and Track Development (1815–25)

In the period 1815–25 continuous progress was made in both locomotive and track design. Initially, rails were made of cast iron in 3ft (0.9m) lengths, the ends butting together in chairs placed on stone blocks or wooden sleepers. In September 1816, George Stephenson and William Losh, a Newcastle ironfounder, patented an improved form of cast-iron rail and chair, details of which are shown in Fig 8. The rail length was increased to about 4ft (1.2m) and the butt joint replaced by a scarfed or half-lapped joint. The rails sat on a chair with convex bearing and a securing bolt passed through the chair lugs and half-laps. They were adopted on the Killingworth colliery railway and improved the efficiency of horse and locomotive traction. The locomotive had only just begun to replace the horse and it took Stephenson a further fifteen years to establish the validity of steam power.

Fig 8 In 1816 George Stephenson and William Losh
replaced the butt rail joint by a lapped joint

An extensive series of trials were made to investigate the influence of track design, wind resistance, friction and gradient on the efficiency of locomotive operations. The trials took place at Killingworth and Hetton. Hetton colliery is situated about 6 miles (9.6km) south of the River Wear. The colliery required a railway to transport coal from the pit head to the river. Stephenson was appointed engineer in 1819 and the line opened in November 1822. Steep gradients precluded the use of locomotives on the whole of the line. There were five self-acting inclines (full wagons drawing empty ones up) and two inclines worked by fixed engines. The locomotives ran at about 4mph (6kph) pulling a load of 64 tons (640kN).

The Hetton and Killingworth lines were inspected by a deputation from the promoters of the Liverpool & Manchester Railway and the railway operations were demonstrated by George Stephenson. An independent report was prepared by Charles Sylvester, a civil engineer, and submitted to the chairman of the committee of the projected Liverpool & Manchester Railway. Sylvester's report referred extensively to the experiments carried out on locomotives at the Killingworth and Hetton collieries and concluded that at their existing state of development, they were a great improvement on the employment of horse power and, more important, they were capable of 'so much improvement'. A maximum gradient of 1 in 360 was recommended as the limit to economic operation of a locomotive on a railway.

The Stockton & Darlington Railway

The juxtaposition of events mitigates against keeping to a precise chronological sequence and it is necessary to go back to 1818 for the origin of the first projection of the Stockton & Darlington Railway. Edward Pease (1767–1858), an influential Quaker, formed a company for the purpose of promoting the Stockton & Darlington Railway with a Welsh engineer, George Overton, employed as surveyor. The name 'Stockton & Darlington Railway' is confusing as the line was built to transport coal from pits to the North and West of Shildon via Darlington, for shipment on the Tees at Stockton (see Fig 9).

Royal assent was given to the first Stockton and Darlington Railway Act on 19 April 1821. On 28 April 1821, Edward Pease received the following letter from George Stephenson:

Killingworth Colliery
April 28th 1821

Sir,

I have been favoured with your letter of the 20th Inst. I am glad to learn that the Bill has passed for the Darlington railway. I am much obliged by the favourable sentiments you express towards me: I shall be happy if I can be of service in carrying out execution of your plans. From the nature of my engagements here and in the neighbourhood, I could not devote the whole of my time to your Railway, but I am willing to undertake to survey and mark out the best line of way within the limits prescribed by the Act of Parliament and also, to assist the Committee with plans and estimates, and in letting to the different contractors such work as they might judge it advisable to do by contract and also to superintend the execution of the work — And I am induced to recommend the whole being done by contract under the superintendence of competent persons appointed by the Committee. Were I to contract for the whole line of Road it would be necessary for me to do so at an advance price upon the sub-contractors, and it would also be necessary for the Committee to have some person to superintend my undertaking. This would be attended with an extra expense, and the Committee would derive no advantage to compensate for it. If you wish it I will wait upon you at Darlington at an early opportunity when I can enter into more particulars as to the remuneration etc, etc.

I remain yours respectfully
GEORGE STEPHENSON

George Overton was eased out of the position of engineer and George Stephenson with the help of his son Robert resurveyed the line and submitted modified proposals more suited to locomotive haulage. In January 1822 Stephenson was appointed engineer at a salary of £660 per annum and commenced work on parts of the line which were not affected by his survey.

The first rails were laid in May 1822 and further Acts of Parliament to sanction Stephenson's modifications to the route received royal assent in 1823 and 1824. It was originally intended that passengers and goods were to be horse-drawn, but a new clause was inserted in the Bill to

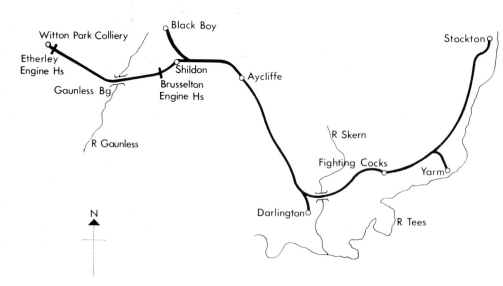

Fig 9 The route of the Stockton & Darlington Railway which was opened in 1825

Plate 10 A working replica of *Locomotion* which is frequently in steam at the Beamish North of England Open Air Museum (*Frances Gibson-Smith*)

allow the use of locomotives. The opening ceremony was on Tuesday 27 September 1825 and although a great success, it was some years before it could be established that steam haulage was cheaper than horse haulage. The first passenger service commenced in October 1825 with a daily horse-drawn coach between Darlington and Stockton. It was not until 1834 that the locomotive replaced the horse for both passenger and goods trains.

The first four locomotives — *Locomotion, Hope, Black Diamond* and *Diligence* — were delivered between September 1825 and May 1826. They were built at the Forth Street works of Robert Stephenson & Co (see page 63). *Locomotion* was constructed to the design of George Stephenson — it weighed 6½ tons (65kN), the driving wheels were 4ft (1.2m) in diameter and the cylinders were 9½in (24cm) x 24in (61cm). The working pressure of the boiler was 50psi. *Locomotion* was withdrawn from service in 1850 and in 1857 was placed on a pedestal outside North Road Station at Darlington. It was moved to a new site under cover at Bank Top Station in 1890. The photographs (Plates 10, 11 and 12) are taken of a working replica of the original which is frequently in steam at Beamish North of England Open Air Museum, Beamish Hall, Stanley, Durham.

Two interesting civil engineering aspects of the Stockton & Darlington Railway are the Gaunless Bridge (for original location see Fig 9) and the design of the track. Gaunless Bridge is reputed to be the first iron railway bridge ever built and was situated on the level section of the line worked by horse haulage between the Etherley and Brusselton inclines. It was designed by George Stephenson and embodies an interesting structural concept — the combination of the arch and chain (Fig 10). The outward thrust of the top compression boom is

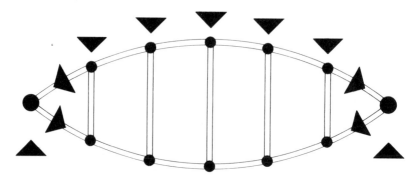

Fig 10 The structural concept of the Gaunless Bridge designed by George Stephenson

Plate 11 *Locomotion* and a train of chaldron wagons with the mine shaft and headgear at the North of England Open Air Museum (*Frances Gibson-Smith*)

Plate 12 The front view of *Locomotion* (*Frances Gibson-Smith*)

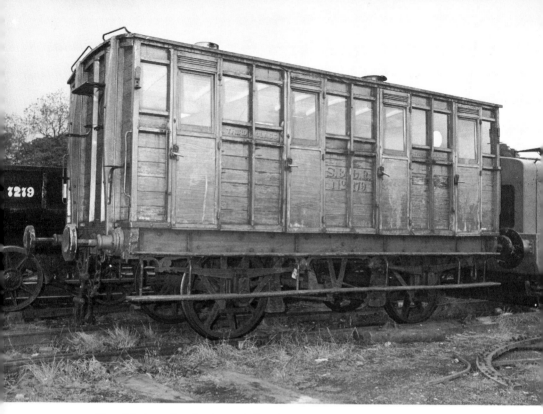

Plate 13 A replica Stockton & Darlington Railway third-class carriage at Beamish (*Frances Gibson-Smith*)

balanced by the inward pull of the bottom tension boom. Wrought iron was used for the curved members (2½in (6cm) diameter) and the verticals were of cast iron, thus demonstrating Stephenson's appreciation of the difference between the properties of wrought and cast iron (see p121). The verticals transmitted the load from the timber deck above and kept the curved wrought-iron bars in shape. Three spans were erected in 1824 by John and Isaac Burrell of Orchard Street, Newcastle. The fourth span was erected in 1825 following damage by flooding and the bridge was brought into use when the line was opened in September 1825. The bridge was dismantled in 1901 and later re-erected at Queen Street Museum, York, for its opening in 1927. Plates 14–17 (pages 42-3) illustrate details of the construction of the bridge and it is now located outside the main hall of the National Railway Museum, Leeman Road, York. There is a chaldron wagon mounted on the timber deck and the bracing system is of particular interest.

It will be recalled that in 1816 Stephenson and Losh patented a cast-iron rail with a length of 4ft (1.2m). Cast-iron rails were rejected by Stephenson for all but four of the 25 mile (40km) single-track route.

The cast-iron rails were 4ft (1.2m) in length and weighed 57½lb/yd (28.52kg/m). For 19 miles (30km) of the track, Stephenson took advantage of John Birkinshaw's patented method of rolling wrought-iron rails in 12ft (3.6m) and 15ft (4.5m) lengths. This demonstrates once again Stephenson's appreciation of the superiority of wrought iron. The wrought-iron rails weighed 28lb/yd (13.88kg/m) and the cost per ton (£12 10s) was about twice that of cast iron (£6 15s). Thus, the cost per mile for wrought- and cast-iron rails was approximately the same (Rolt). The Birkinshaw rail, c1825 is illustrated in Fig 11. To the west of Darlington, the rails were supported on stone sleeper blocks (18in [46cm] x 14in [35cm] x 8in [20cm]) which weighed 140lb (63kg) each. As an economy measure, wooden blocks (oak, 18in [46cm] x 7in [18cm] x 5in [13cm] were used in place of stone blocks for the remainder of the line. Cross sleepers were not used, presumably because extensive horse-hauled traffic was anticipated.

Fifteen months before the Stockton & Darlington Railway was completed, George Stephenson, at a salary of £1,000 a year, was appointed as engineer to a project for constructing a railway between Liverpool and Manchester. Although Stephenson's unique experience and talent made him the obvious choice for the world's first inter-city railway, he was shortly to undergo merciless humiliation by the legal profession which would have defeated a lesser man. Further, his son was unable to support him as he was working in South America (see Chapter 8).

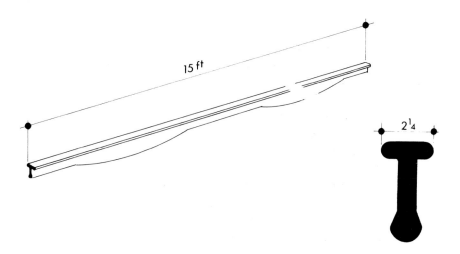

15 ft

2¼

Fig 11 Birkinshaw's wrought-iron rail rolled in 15ft (4.5m) lengths in fish-belly form

Plates 14, 15, 16 and 17 Views of the Gaunless Bridge with cast- and wrought-iron components (*Frances Gibson-Smith*)

Liverpool & Manchester Railway

Space permits only the briefest description of the Liverpool & Manchester Railway which celebrated its 150th anniversary in 1980. The history, construction and the Rainhill trials are described at length elsewhere (see Bibliography). At the beginning of the nineteenth century, the growth of industry in and around Manchester and the expansion of the port of Liverpool were hampered by a grossly inefficient transport system between Lancashire's principal towns. The possibility of building a railway was an obvious attraction to businessmen, except those with canal and coaching interests. Between 1800 and 1820, a number of proposals were put forward for building a wagonway or railway between Liverpool and Manchester, but the first serious attempt was made by William James (1771–1837). William James had colliery and land interests and in 1821 was appointed to carry out a preliminary survey. He consulted George Stephenson at Killingworth and this was followed by a second survey in which he was assisted by Robert Stephenson. Pressure of work prevented James from completing the survey and after some delay, George Stephenson replaced James as engineer in the summer of 1824. Throughout the survey, Stephenson encountered vicious opposition from the landed, coaching and canal factions. The petition for a Bill was presented to the House of Commons in February 1825. In the witness box George Stephenson's lack of formal education was exploited brutally by the opposing counsel, Edward Alderson, and the following is an extract from the evidence (F. Ferneyhough):

ALDERSON: This is the most absurd scheme that ever entered into the head of a man to conceive . . . my learned friends almost endeavoured to stop my examination . . . but I had rather have the exhibition of Mr Stephenson in that box. I say he never had a plan . . . I do not believe he is capable of making one . . . He is either ignorant or something else which I will not mention . . .

The cross-examination also revealed surveying errors and guessed estimates and inevitably the Bill was thrown out after several months of committee sessions. In June 1825, Stephenson was relieved of his post of engineer to the railway to prevent further embarrassment and the railway board approached a distinguished civil engineering family, the Rennies. John Rennie (1761–1821) built Waterloo and Southwark bridges and designed the new London Bridge which his son John completed. John Rennie and his brother George (1791–1866) were primarily involved in the construction of canals and bridges but had also

44

planned a route for a railway between London and Brighton. The survey was made by Charles Blacker Vignoles (1793–1875). The Rennies convinced the railway board of their competence to undertake the work and Vignoles was appointed to survey Stephenson's route. Adjustments were made to appease landowners and others and Vignoles and Rennie were better equipped than Stephenson to handle parliamentary committees.

In particular, Vignoles had originally trained for the law and this must have been of great benefit in dealing with Alderson's penetrating cross-examination. The Bill received royal assent in May 1826, but the Rennie brothers were not appointed as engineers for the construction of the railway. There was continued pressure to involve Stephenson in the construction but the Rennies were adamant that he should not be involved in the civil engineering works. They had no objection, however, to his becoming involved with the locomotive department. This was not acceptable to the board and in July 1826 George Stephenson was appointed as principal engineer with Vignoles as an engineer. It was not a happy relationship and lasted about six months — Vignoles resigned in February 1827. Vignoles made a significant contribution to the history of railway engineering and in 1837 introduced the flat-bottomed rail section which is now standard throughout the world. In later years the relationship between Stephenson and Vignoles improved through mutual consultations on a number of projects.

Stephenson was left free to build the line his own way. The Rennies' proposal of a 5ft 6in gauge was altered to the Stockton & Darlington gauge of 4ft 8½in clear between the rails. The route and the gradients involved are shown in Figs 12 and 13. It will be recalled that Charles Sylvester's report recommended a maximum gradient of 1 in 360 for efficient operation of locomotives. This is exceeded at three points — the Whiston and Sutton inclines (1 in 96) and at the tunnel from Wapping to Edgehill (1 in 48). Stationary engines were used to haul the trains through the tunnel but it was found that the locomotives could negotiate the 1 in 96 gradient.

Construction of the track involved further development from that adopted for the Stockton & Darlington Railway. The 15ft (4.5m) long wrought-iron rails were maintained with five equal fish-bellied spans, but the weight was increased to 35lb/yd (17.36kg/m). The rails were seated in cast-iron chairs with a side rib and secured by means of a key on the outer side of the rail (Fig 14). The chairs were spiked into split oak or larch logs 8-9ft (2.4-2.7m) long and 10in (2.5cm) in diameter. In

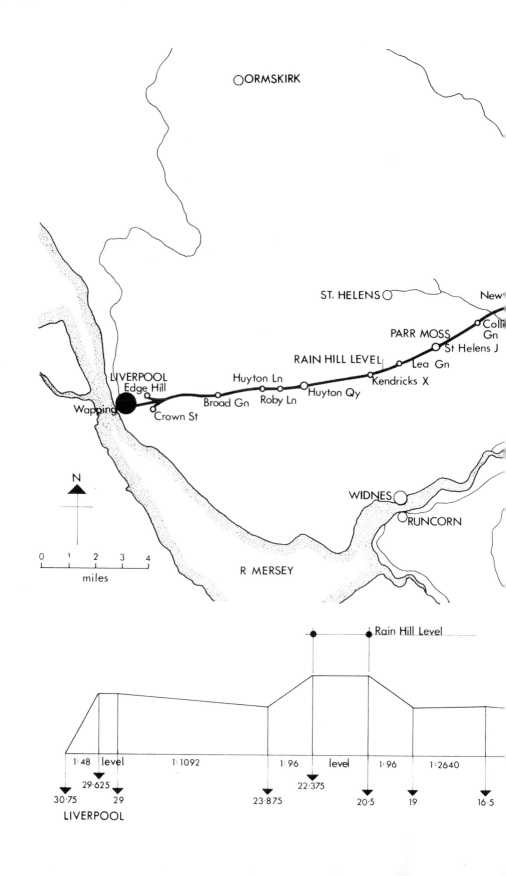

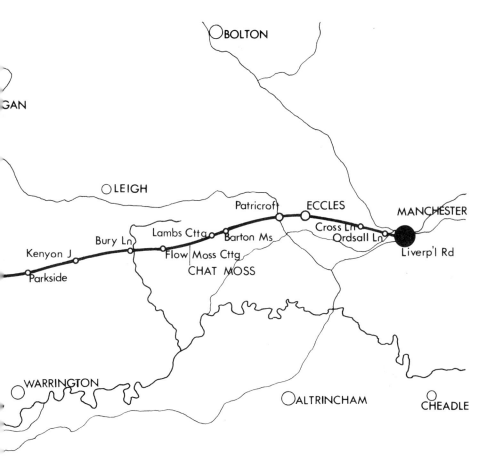

Fig 12 The route of the Liverpool & Manchester Railway

Fig 13 The gradients of the Liverpool & Manchester Railway

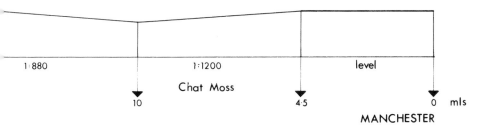

Fig 14 George Stephenson's wrought-iron fish-bellied rails for the Liverpool & Manchester Railway

cuttings, it was considered that the timber would rot owing to the collection of water and the timber sleepers were replaced by stone blocks.

The scale of the civil engineering works on the route has been over-shadowed by the significance of the Rainhill trials (see p54) in relation to establishing the viability of the steam locomotive. In contrast to Smeaton, Telford and the Rennies, George Stephenson's reputation stemmed from his work on the development of locomotives rather than on civil engineering works. However, civil engineering is an essential part of railway construction, and in order to complete the Liverpool & Manchester Railway, Stephenson and his assistants were involved in the construction of over sixty bridges. As we have seen, the construc-tion of the Gaunless Bridge on the Stockton & Darlington Railway demonstrated his appreciation of the difference between the properties of wrought and cast iron and also his understanding of the structural action of arch and chain bridges.

Another significant structure was a skew arch bridge towards the end of the Haggerleases branch line, opened in 1830. The bridge has been demolished. It was necessary for the masons to construct a full-size timber model in order to provide a suitable pattern from which the

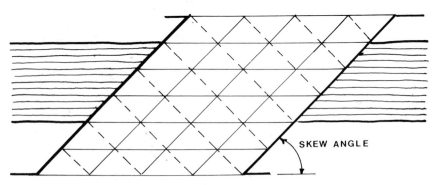

Fig 15 It was predicted that the skew bridge on the Haggerleases branch would collapse, but it carried far heavier weights than its designer intended. The developed plan of the arch was divided into a grid and the brick course lines superimposed by diagonals bisecting the grid squares

48

stone courses could be built up. In a conventional arch, the segments or voussoirs are placed on timber centering and built out at right angles to the line of abutments, the joints in the stones or bricks forming a right angle with the line of thrust (see *Brunel's Britain*). If the arch is built at an angle (skew) to the line of the abutments and the courses constructed as above, the line of the thrust will not be at right angles to the joints as it runs parallel to the face of the arch (Fig 15). If the oblique angle is too large, instability can result. The most common solution to the problem was known as the 'spiral method' (R. S. Fitzgerald), devised by William Chapman (1749–1832) and explained in Rees' *Cyclopedia* (1813–14). The curved form of the soffit of the skew arch was developed into a plane form and divided into a grid. Diagonals were drawn on the grid which was then transferred on to the arch centering (see also Chapter 3). The most celebrated of George Stephenson's skew arches is the 54ft (16m) span Rainhill Bridge (Plate 18), completed at the end of 1828. This bridge is in use today and a wooden model was used to facilitate its construction. Another example of skew-bridge construction is the bridge over the River Irwell, close to Liverpool Road Station, Manchester, which consists of two brick arches with ashlar facings.

Plate 18 A lithograph of the skew bridge at Rainhill, Crane, 1830 (*Science Museum, London*)

Plate 19 The viaduct over the Sankey canal; lithograph by W. Benson *(Science Museum, London)*

Although not of skew form, the most impressive of George Stephenson's bridge works on the line is the Sankey viaduct over the Sankey canal (Plate 19). The nine 50ft (15m) span arches are constructed principally of brick and the piers are supported on timber piles. It is surprising that George Stephenson's background of locomotive engineering and track design did not encourage him to make more extensive use of cast and wrought iron on the Liverpool & Manchester Railway. The ingenious arch/chain solution for the Gaunless Viaduct was not repeated, but cast iron was used in the construction of Water Street Bridge adjacent to the station and warehouse (1830) at Liverpool Road, Manchester.

In the use of cast iron, George Stephenson leaned heavily on the expertise of William Fairbairn (1789–1861) and Eaton Hodgkinson (1789–1874). This association was continued by his son Robert in the construction of the Britannia and Conwy tubular bridges (see Chapter 6). George Stephenson's friendship with William Fairbairn dates back to 1803, and in the 1820s Fairbairn and Hodgkinson worked together on the development of cast-iron beams, making use of Fairbairn's testing facilities. Fairbairn utilised cast iron in inverted T-form in the construction of mill buildings. This type of beam had its origins in the late eighteenth century as a means of providing support to brick segmental arch floors. The bottom flange was used as a springing point for

50

the construction of the brick arches. It is fortunate that use was not made of the published information available at the time. In 1822, Thomas Tredgold (1788–1829) published a book which included some misleading information on the properties of cast iron. Based on tests on small cast-iron sections (1in [25mm] x 1in [25mm]), Tredgold indicated that a factor of safety of about 3 would be achieved with a working stress in bending under the full design load of about 6.8 tons/in² (104 N/mm²) (R. J. M. Sutherland). This level of stress suggests the use of an I-section with top and bottom flanges of approximately equal area. Luckily, Fairbairn from historical precedence of use of an inverted T-beam in mill floors, Hodgkinson from tests to determine the option form for cast-iron sections and Stephenson from an intuitive understanding of the weakness of cast iron, did not make use of Tredgold's recommenda-tions. The form of the cast-iron sections used in the construction of Water Street Bridge is shown in Fig 16. It was built at a skew angle of 39° with the main beams of clear span 24ft 9in (7.5m), at 13ft 6in (4.1m) centres, connected by secondary beams at 2ft 9in (0.8m) centres (R. S. Fitzgerald). The secondary beams supported brick arches and thus the constructional details resembled that of mill floors. The ratio of bottom flange to top flange area is 2.5 and 3.8 for the primary and secondary beams respectively, necessitated by the increased area of material required to resist tension. The primary beams were parabolic in longitudinal profile as were the bottom flanges in plan, and thus the

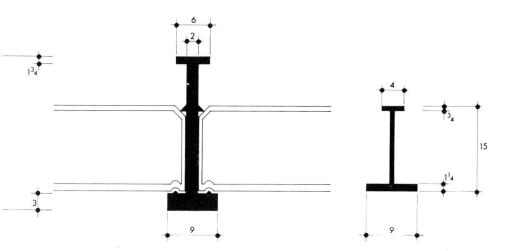

Fig 16 The primary and secondary cast-iron beams of the Water Street Bridge. Note the difference in top and bottom flange areas

maximum cross-sectional area of material was provided at midspan where the bending effect is greatest. This attempt to modify the section geometry indicated an advanced level of understanding of structural form and the bulk of the credit can be attributed to Hodgkinson. Further development of the inverted T-profile is discussed in Chapter 5 together with Robert Stephenson's lack of understanding of the composite action of cast-iron T-beams and wrought-iron tie bars which led to the collapse of the bridge over the River Dee at Chester. Water Street Bridge was demolished in 1905 but the adjacent warehouse and station are currently being restored to form the home of the North Western Museum of Science & Technology.

The most controversial aspect of the construction work was Stephenson's decision to take the line across Chat Moss bog, for a distance of 5 miles (8km). The peat bog lies to the north side of the River Irwell and is of roughly triangular form with the line crossing it at its widest point. The bog was higher in the centre than at its edges and the depth varied from a few feet to 35ft (10.6m). The line was originally staked out by Vignoles with the aid of planks laid on the bog. Stephenson appointed John Dixon as resident engineer for this section of the line and on his first inspection he slipped off a plank and sank to his knees. He was rescued by workmen but it was not a promising start to providing a stable foundation over a length of 5 miles (8km). Stephenson's proposal was that the track could be supported on a floating raft and the first stage was to form a footpath of heather from which a single-line 3ft gauge wooden track was laid. This supported wagons carrying the fill material. Previous experience of land reclamation work on the southeast corner of the Moss possibly led to the method of filling the bog with timber laid in herring-bone fashion with spoil sandwiched between. Another technique was to build up with moss, heather and brushwood bundles which were topped with earth, aggregates and cinders. By the end of 1829, one line of track had been laid across Chat Moss. Dixon later became chief engineer of the Liverpool & Manchester Railway.

The year 1829 was a testing one in George Stephenson's life — the civil engineering aspects of the line were more or less under control, but the method of traction had not been resolved. Thus Stephenson had still to establish the viability of the locomotive for carrying goods and passengers between Liverpool and Manchester. The use of cable haulage with the motive power being provided by stationary engines was still a real possibility. At a meeting in april 1829, the directors of the Liverpool & Manchester decided that:

a premium of £500 be advertised for a Locomotive Engine which shall be a decided improvement on those now in use, as respects the consumption of smoke, increased speed, adequate power and moderate weight, the particulars of which shall be specified in detail by the Preparation Committee . . .

The stipulations and conditions are laid out below.

1829. GRAND COMPETITION OF LOCOMOTIVES ON THE
LIVERPOOL AND MANCHESTER RAILWAY

STIPULATIONS & CONDITIONS
ON WHICH THE DIRECTORS OF THE LIVERPOOL AND MANCHESTER RAILWAY OFFER A PREMIUM OF £500 FOR THE MOST IMPROVED LOCOMOTIVE ENGINE.

I   The said Engine must "effectually consume its own smoke," according to the provisions of the Railway Act, 7th Geo. IV.

II   The Engine, if it weighs Six Tons, must be capable of drawing after it, day by day, on a well-constructed Railway, on a level plane, a Train of Carriages of the gross weight of Twenty Tons, including the Tender and Water Tank, at the rate of Ten Miles per Hour, with a pressure of steam in the boiler not exceeding Fifty Pounds on the square inch.

III There must be Two Safety Valves, one of which must be completely out of reach or control of the Engine-man, and neither of which must be fastened down while the Engine is working.

IV   The Engine and Boiler must be supported on Springs, and rest on Six Wheels; and the height from the ground to the top of the Chimney must not exceed Fifteen Feet.

V   The weight of the Machine, WITH ITS COMPLEMENT OF WATER in the Boiler, must, at most, not exceed Six Tons, and a Machine of less weight will be preferred if it draw AFTER it a PROPORTIONATE weight; and if the weight of the Engine, etc., do not exceed FIVE TONS, then the gross weight to be drawn need not exceed Fifteen Tons; and in that proportion for Machines of still smaller weight — provided that the Engine, etc., shall still be on six wheels, unless the weight (as above) be reduced to Four Tons and a Half, or under, in which case the Boiler, etc., may be placed on four wheels. And the Company shall be at liberty to put the Boiler, Fire Tube, Cylinders, etc., to the test of a pressure of water not exceeding 150 Pounds per square inch, without being answerable for any damage the Machine may receive in consequence.

VI   There must be a Mercurial Gauge affixed to the Machine, with Index Rod, showing the Steam Pressure above 45 Pounds per square inch; and constructed to blow out a Pressure of 60 Pounds per inch.

VII The Engine to be delivered complete for trial, at the Liverpool end of the Railway, not later than the 1st of October next.

VIII The price of the Engine which may be accepted, not to exceed £550, delivered on the Railway; and any Engine not approved to be taken back by the Owner.

N.B. — The Railway Company will provide the ENGINE TENDER with a supply of Water and Fuel, for the experiment. The distance within the Rails is four feet eight inches and a half.

The Stephensons entered 0-2-2 locomotive (No 19 Travelling Engine, *Rocket*, originally named the *Premium Engine*) upon which work commenced in April 1829 at the Forth Street works, Newcastle. The design was modelled on No 12 Travelling Engine, *Lancashire Witch*, completed in July 1828. Technical details of the *Rocket*, which had two outside inclined cylinders, are given below:

Driving wheel diameter	4ft 8½in (143.5cm)
Trailing wheel diameter	2ft 6in (76.2cm)
Boiler	6ft (182.8cm) long, 3ft 4in (101.6cm) in diameter containing 25 copper tubes, 3in (7.6cm) in diameter
Cylinders diameter and stroke	8in (20.3cm) x 17in (43.2cm)
Working pressure	50lb sq/in (3.51kg/sq cm)
Weight in working order	4¼ tons (42.5kN)
Livery	Yellow and black, chimney white

The most significant technical development in this design was the use of a multi-tube boiler. Hot gases from the firebox pass through the tubes which are surrounded by water in the boiler, thus achieving a much larger heating surface. The multi-tube boiler was patented by a French engineer and scientist, Marc Séguin (1786–1875), in 1827 and the idea was suggested to the Stephensons by Henry Booth, secretary of the Liverpool & Manchester Railway. Robert Stephenson was responsible for the design and construction of the *Rocket* and it underwent trials at Killingworth in early September 1829. The partially dismantled engine was transported by road and ship to Liverpool via the Solway Firth. The trials took place on the Rainhill level sandwiched between the Whiston and Sutton inclines. The official trials were commenced on 8 October 1829 and full details are given elsewhere (Ferneyhough and Carlson). Briefly, the *Rocket* was the only locomotive to fulfil all the conditions and in the final of the forty 1¾ mile (2.8km) runs, it achieved an average speed of 24mph (38.6kph) with a full load of 12¾ tons (127kN) — three times its weight. George Stephenson's triumph was completed when he demonstrated that the *Rocket* could negotiate the Whiston incline with ease. With the official opening of the line on 15 September 1830, Stephenson had established the validity of a means of traction that did not become obsolete until the demise of the steam engine some 140 years later.

The Stephensons' railway, both in civil and mechanical engineering terms, was developed continuously from 1815, and in 1830, the 2-2-0 *Planet* (Plate 21), the ninth locomotive built by the Stephensons for the

Plate 20 The remains of Stephenson's *Rocket*, 1829, in the Science Museum, London
(Science Museum, London)

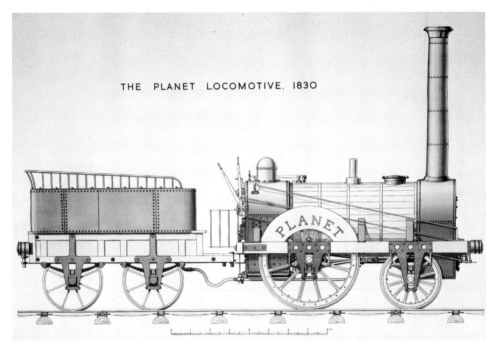

THE PLANET LOCOMOTIVE, 1830

Plate 21 A Science Museum scale drawing of the 2–2–0 *Planet*, 1830, which incorporated all the features of the 'modern' steam locomotive *(Science Museum, London)*

Liverpool & Manchester Railway, incorporated the essential features of the 'modern' steam engine from which there has been little fundamental development. These features were:

1 Horizontal cylinders
2 A multi-tubular boiler
3 The use of the blast of the exhaust
   steam to create a draught for the fire

The technical details of *Planet* were as follows (G. Drysdale Dempsey):

Driving wheel diameter	5ft (152.4cm)
Leading wheel diameter	3ft (91.4cm)
Boiler	6ft 6in long (198.2cm), 3ft (91.4cm) in diameter containing 129 tubes $1\frac{5}{8}$in (4.13cm) diameter
Heating surface	firebox: $37\frac{1}{4}$ft^2 (3.46m^2); tubes: 370ft^2 (34.4m^2)
Cylinders: diameter x stroke	11in (28cm) x 16in (41cm)
Weight in working order	9 tons (90kN)
Working pressure	50 psi (3.51kg/sq cm)

Fig 17 A selection of uniform depth rails used in comparative trials

The cylinders were placed horizontally inside the smokebox and the external wooden frame was strengthened by metal plates. In December 1830, on its first trial, the *Planet* took a 76 ton (760kN) train from Liverpool to Manchester in 2 hours 39 minutes at a maximum speed of 15¼mph (24.5kph). The tractive effort was nearly twice that of the *Rocket*.

In 1832, George Stephenson commenced a series of comparative tests to establish the best form of rail and track structure (M. C. Duffy). The weights ranged from 50lb/yd (24.80kg/m) to 75lb/yd (37.2kg/m) and it was established that constant cross-section rail was the best form and it was easier to roll than the fish-belly form. A selection of types used in comparative trials is shown in Fig 17.

A young actress, Fanny Kemble, was invited by George Stephenson to ride on the footplate of one of his engines and gave a charming description of a ride on an early steam engine:

We were introduced to the little engine which was to drag us along the rails. She (for they mak the curious little fire horses all mares) consisted of a boiler, a stove, a small platform, a bench and behind the bench a barrel containing enough water to prevent her from being thirsty for 15 miles — the whole machine not bigger than a common fire engine. She goes upon two wheels which are her feet and are moved by bright steel legs called pistons: these are propelled by steam and in proportion as more steam is applied to the upper extremities of these pistons, the faster they move the wheels: and when it is desirable to diminish the speed the steam, which unless suffered to escape would burst the boiler, evaporates through a safety valve into the air.

Plate 22 Stockton & Darlington Railway composite carriage No 59 of 1846 in the National Railway Museum Collection. The three- compartment, four wheel design was typical of the early years of railways. The guard sat on the roof amongst the luggage and had to descend to apply the brakes whenever the driver whistled such an instruction (*Frances Gibson-Smith*)

The reins, bit and bridle of this wonderful beast is a small steel handle which applies or withdraws the steam from the piston. The coals, which are its oats, were under the bench, and there was a small glass tube fixed to the boiler, with water in it, which indicates by its fullness or emptiness when the creature wants water. This snorting little animal was then harnessed to our carriage and Mr Stephenson, having taken me on the engine with him, started at about ten miles an hour.

You cannot conceive what that sensation of cutting the air was: the motion was as smooth as possible, too. I could either have read or written; as it was I stood up and with my bonnet off drank the air before me. When I closed my eyes this sensation of flying was quite delightful; yet, strange as it was, I had a perfect sense of security . . .

(JOHN THOMAS, *Popular Archaeology*)

In the 1830s George Stephenson was heavily involved in surveying and supervising the construction of numerous railways, particularly in the north Midlands. By the end of the decade, however, his son Robert played an increasingly prominent role in the building of new railways, in particular, the London & Birmingham Railway. In the 1840s George Stephenson lived in virtual retirement while his son became heavily immersed in the construction of the Chester & Holyhead and the York, Newcastle & Berwick railways. Stephenson's last home was Tapton House, Chesterfield, which is now a school. Its large grounds enabled him to indulge in more rural pursuits which were all tackled with great vigour. There were numerous visitors to Tapton House and typical of Stephenson's reaction to a young man's request for advice on becoming an engineer was:

you will, I hope Mr – , excuse me; I am a plain spoken person, and am sorry to see a nice looking and rather clever young man like you disfigured with that fine patterned waistcoat, and all these chains and fang-dangs. If I, sir, had bothered my head with such things at your age, I would not have been where I am now.

(SMILES)

Plate 23 George Stephenson's last home, Tapton House, on a hill overlooking Chesterfield in Derbyshire now used as a school (*Frances Gibson-Smith*)

Stephenson's observations on the realities of life are most revealing:

'I will only say this, that of all the powers above and under the earth, there seems to me to be no power so great as the gift of the gab.' His observation on the power of a woman is on the title verso.

Throughout his life, Stephenson suffered from a lack of formal education, but it is a measure of the man that he achieved such status without it. Throughout the construction of the Liverpool & Manchester Railway, his methods were severely criticised, with some justification, by leading civil engineers. In earlier editions of Smiles' biography, it was implied that Stephenson's qualifications for becoming a member of the Institution of Civil Engineers (founded in 1818) were in doubt. The matter has been put in perspective by L. T. C. Rolt.

It is highly unlikely that as late as 1846 Stephenson would apply for membership and even more unlikely that he would be refused, as his son was a member of the council. In 1847 a group of engineers proposed

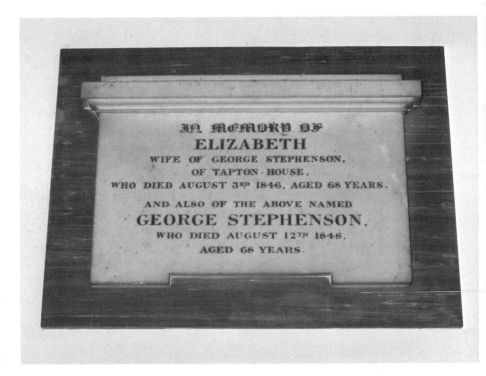

Plate 24 A memorial plaque to George Stephenson and his wife Elizabeth in Holy Trinity Church, Chesterfield (*Frances Gibson-Smith*)

Plate 25 George Stephenson was buried at Holy Trinity Church, Chesterfield, in August 1848 (*Frances Gibson-Smith*)

the formation of the Institution of Mechanical Engineers and at a general meeting held at the Queen's Hotel, Birmingham, George Stephenson was elected the first president. The objectives were

to enable mechanics and engineers engaged in the different manufactories, railways and other establishments in the Kingdom to meet and correspond, and by a mutual exchange of ideas respecting improvements in the various branches of mechanical science, to increase their knowledge and give an impulse to inventions likely to be useful to the world.

The objective of the Institution of Civil Engineers was 'the acquisition of that species of knowledge which constitutes the profession of a civil engineer'. Thomas Telford (1757–1834) was the first president.

Prior to the founding of the Institution of Civil Engineers, a Society of Civil Engineers, now called the Smeatonian Society, was formed in 1771 by practising engineers who had already attained some eminence. Amongst the ten founders were John Smeaton (1724–92) and William Jessop (1744–1814).

George Stephenson's second wife, Elizabeth, died in 1845 and he was married for the third time in early 1848 to his housekeeper, Ellen Gregory. Following two attacks of pleurisy, George Stephenson died on 12 August 1848. He was buried at Holy Trinity Church, Chesterfield (Plate 25), and there is a simple memorial tablet on the floor at the foot of the altar. There is another plaque in memory of Elizabeth and George Stephenson (Plate 24).

2

ROBERT STEPHENSON

I sometimes feel very uneasy about my position. My courage at times almost fails me and I fear that some fine morning my reputation may break under me like an eggshell.

(ROBERT STEPHENSON)

The first year of Robert Stephenson's life was spent at Willington Quay, and in 1804 the family moved to the cottage at Killingworth (see Plate 9). His education at the village school in Long Benton, Mr Bruce's school at Percy Street in Newcastle, study at the Newcastle Literary and Philosophical Institute and a six-month period at Edinburgh University are described elsewhere. Prior to attending the University, Robert served an apprenticeship at Killingworth pit under the head viewer, Nicholas Wood. The apprenticeship commenced in the summer of 1819 after he had left Mr Bruce's school. Robert also assisted his father with survey work on the Stockton & Darlington Railway. On leaving Edinburgh University in April 1823, Robert Stephenson was shortly to become involved with a project which would stretch both his practical and theoretical experience — a new locomotive works.

In June 1823, Robert Stephenson accepted the position of managing partner of Robert Stephenson & Co. The other partners were George Stephenson, Edward Pease, Thomas Richardson and Michael Longridge (M. R. Bailey). It was apparent to the partners, who were convinced of an auspicious future for railways, that there would be an increased demand for locomotives, winding engines, track, and so on. The company commenced trading in July and a factory was built in South Street (off Forth Street), Newcastle.

A marketing exercise was undertaken by George and Robert Stephenson which involved trips to London and Ireland. In London the reputation of the Stephensons became known to the Mexican Mining Association and a major order was anticipated. Early customers included the Stockton & Darlington Railway and the Stockton Steam Boat Company. In January 1824, Robert Stephenson senior (b 10

March 1788, see family tree), Robert's uncle, accepted an offer to work for the Mexican Mining Association which he subsequently declined but Robert himself accepted a similar post with the Colombian Mining Association. This decision caused serious disruption in the partnership as the company was already over-committed, but Robert could not be persuaded to change his mind. His reasons for leaving England have been the subject of much speculation and it must be said that his father could not have been the easiest of persons to work with, to say the least. A number of reasons may have contributed to the decision and possibly one of them was that he had no great liking for the day-to-day operations

Plate 26 A middle-aged Robert Stephenson (*National Portrait Gallery*)

of a locomotive factory. His father was busy with matters elsewhere and it is significant that in later years, Robert's interests leaned more towards the civil engineering aspects of railway construction. Robert left the company a year after it was formed and did not return to Newcastle until the end of 1827 (see Chapter 8). In the period 1824–7 the company went through difficult times and much of George Stephenson's time was spent on the Liverpool & Manchester Railway. In 1828 Robert embarked on a reappraisal of locomotive design which culminated in the construction of the *Rocket* (see p54). The company's affairs prospered and locomotives were exported to France and North America. Business was not confined to locomotive production: for example, three high-pressure winding engines were ordered for the Canterbury & Whitstable Railway.

Canterbury & Whitstable Railway

The first survey for the proposed Canterbury & Whitstable Railway was carried out by William James in April 1823. Subsequently, James faded from the scene and George Stephenson was consulted. The line was then surveyed by two of Stephenson's assistants, Joseph Locke and John Dixon. The final plans were prepared by John Dixon (Rolt), and Robert took over from his father as engineer to the line. The line was opened on 3 May 1830 and thus its claim to fame is that it operated passenger trains hauled by locomotives prior to the opening of the Liverpool & Manchester Railway. However, fixed engines were used on 4 of its 6 mile (9.6km) length (see Fig 18). The first locomotive brought into service, *Invicta*, was built by Robert Stephenson & Co and delivered by sea from Newcastle to Whitstable harbour. Robert Stephenson supervised the works from Newcastle with trips to Canterbury via London to meet the object of his affections, Fanny Sanderson. They were married on 17 June 1829 (see family tree).

Leicester & Swannington Railway

Another example of Robert's ability to take over railway engineering works from his father was the Leicester & Swannington Railway. The need to transport coal from pits located 10–15 miles (16–24km) to the west of Leicester provided the impetus to promote the construction of a railway from Leicester to Swannington. A local colliery owner had been impressed by the Stockton & Darlington Railway and George

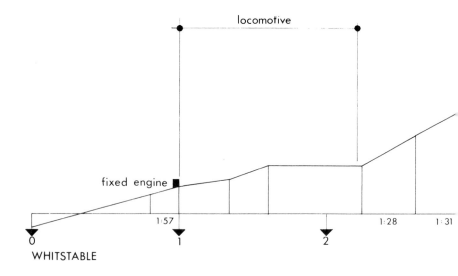

Fig 18 The gradients of the Canterbury & Whitstable Railway

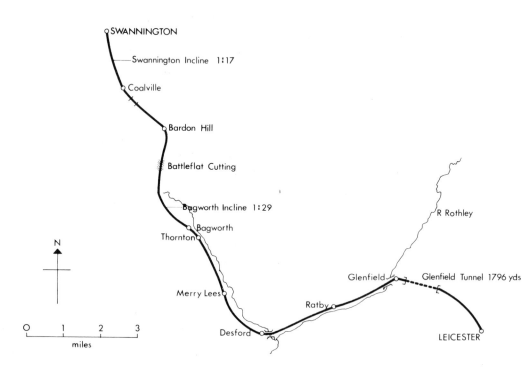

Fig 19 The route of the Leicester & Swannington Railway

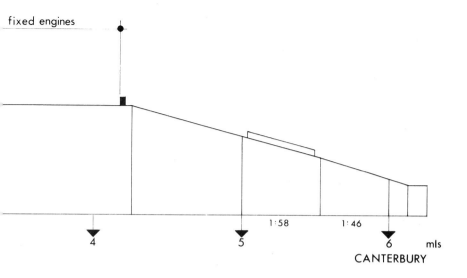

fixed engines

1:58   1:46

4   5   6   mls
CANTERBURY

Stephenson was consulted at Liverpool while working on the Liverpool & Manchester Railway. A provisional committee was formed in February 1829 (C. R. Clinker) and Robert Stephenson was appointed as engineer. The Act received royal assent in May 1830 and the works included ten bridges, two inclines (Bagworth 1 in 29 and Swannington 1 in 17) and the 1,796yd (1,642m) long Glenfield Tunnel (all Fig 19).

Problems arose with the tunnel resulting from faulty trial borings. The contractor was under the impression that he would be working in stone throughout, but a 500yd (457m) length of sand was encountered. Robert Stephenson directed that the tunnel would have to be brick-lined throughout, which almost doubled the cost. It is ventilated by ten shafts, two of which are in the gardens of private dwellings (C. R. Clinker).

The Bagworth incline was not worked with a stationary engine but on a self-acting counterbalance principle. The 946yd (873m) incline of 1 in 29 fell in the direction of movement of the loaded coal wagons. The reverse occurred at Swannington where the movement of loaded wagons was against the grade so a stationary engine was required at the top. The wagons were hauled up the incline (1 in 17) by means of a cable on a drum driven from the engine. The engine ceased working in 1947 and has now been completely restored with a new flywheel. It is housed in the main hall of the National Railway Museum, York (see Plates 27 and 28) where it can be made to rotate by an electric motor.

67

Plates 27 and 28 The Swannington winding engine restored with a new flywheel at the National Railway Museum, York. A photograph of the winding house may be seen in the background (*Frances Gibson-Smith*)

The first six locomotives were ordered from Robert Stephenson & Co, the first of which, the *Comet*, was handed over on 5 May 1832 (C. R. Clinker). It drew the inaugural train from Leicester twelve days later. The Stephensons' engines were not successful, possibly because the power required to pull heavily loaded coal wagons was underestimated. The permanent way specification was similar to that initially adopted for the Liverpool & Manchester Railway (see p45). Details are as follows (C. R. Clinker):

Fish-belly rails 15ft (4.5m) long, weight 35lb/yd (17.36kg/m) midspan depth 3½in (89mm) and at the chairs 2½in (64mm). Rails secured by wrought-iron keys 10in (254mm) long. In cuttings the rails were supported at 3ft (0.9m) centres on diagonally placed stone blocks 1ft 8in sq (50.8cm sq) and 10in (254mm) deep. Elsewhere the rails were supported on timber sleepers 8ft 6in (2.6m) long.

The Stanhope & Tyne Railway

While Robert Stephenson was engaged upon construction of the Leicester & Swannington Railway as engineer, he agreed to act as a consultant to the promoters of a railway some 140 miles (225km) north of Leicester. The scheme for the Stanhope & Tyne Railway evolved from a demand for limestone which was used in the production of iron. It was proposed that the limestone at Stanhope, about 25 miles (40km) south west of Newcastle, could be transported by rail to the deep-water port at South Shields on the south side of the Tyne estuary. The route via Rowley, Consett, Stanley and Washington to South Shields required negotiation of some difficult terrain on the Pennine uplands. The first section of the line, running north from Stanhope, passed between Collier Law and Bolt's Law (1,773ft [540m]) and required two steep inclines worked by stationary engines. The 34 mile (54.7km) route was completed in 1834 and sources of traction were the horse, stationary engines, inclined planes and the locomotive. Less than 30 per cent of the length of the line was worked by locomotives.

Unfortunately, Robert Stephenson paid little attention to the commercial viability of the line and agreed to accept shares in lieu of his consultancy fee (L. T. C. Rolt). The application to Parliament for an Act of Incorporation was not made and the high rents charged by landowners for way-leaves, together with poor revenue, eventually brought about the financial collapse of the company. By 1840, Stephenson was forced to take positive action and a new company, the Pontop & South Shields Railway was formed. In order to contribute £20,000 to the company's capital of £400,000, Robert Stephenson was compelled to sell to his father a half share in his interest in the Forth Street locomotive works at Newcastle. The limeworks at Stanhope and the western section of the line were sold off and use was made of a short section of the Poptop & South Shields Railway by the newly incorporated Newcastle & Darlington Junction Railway which was backed by George Hudson (1800–71), the 'Railway King'.

Hudson was born in York and achieved commercial success as a draper prior to investing a bequest of £30,000 in railway shares. He became the Lord Mayor of York in 1837 and was appointed chairman of the York & North Midland Railway. Hudson was obsessed with making York a great railway centre ('mak' all t' railways cum t' York') and he became involved with George Stephenson who planned linking the Thames and the Tyne via Birmingham, Leeds and York. However,

Stephenson was persuaded by Hudson to join his North Midland line with the York & North Midland Railway at Normanton, about 10 miles (16km) southeast of Leeds. Thus the route from London to York and beyond would avoid Leeds, putting great emphasis on York as an important railway centre. By the middle of 1840, it was possible to travel by train from Euston to York, albeit by an indirect route of about 220 miles (354km). Four years later, the Thames and the Tyne were linked by the extension of the line from York via Darlington Junction, the stone viaduct at Penshaw crossing the Wear Valley and a short section of the Pontop and South Shields line, reaching the Tyne at the Gateshead terminus. Bridging the Tyne to connect Newcastle and Gateshead was not achieved until 1850 (see Chapter 7).

Robert Stephenson's responsibilities in connection with the Canterbury & Whitstable Railway, the Leicester & Swannington Railway and the Stanhope & Tyne Railway and subsequent works between Darlington and Gateshead were minimal compared with those incurred in the construction of the 112 mile (180km) London-Birmingham line.

The London & Birmingham Railway

In September 1833, Robert Stephenson was appointed chief engineer to the London & Birmingham Railway and the magnitude of this project necessitated a move to London. Samuel Smiles compared the scale of the undertaking with the building of the Great Pyramid of Egypt and observed that 'the English railway was constructed in the face of every conceivable obstruction and difficulty, by a company of private individuals out of their resources, without the aid of Government or the contribution of one farthing of public money'.

The estimate laid before Parliament for the cost of constructing the line was as follows (T. Roscoe):

Excavations and embankments	£179,000
Tunnelling	250,286
Masonry	350,574
Rails, chairs, etc	212,940
Blocks and sleepers	102,960
Ballasting and laying rails	102,960
Fencing	76,032
Land	250,000
Water stations and pumps	3,600
Offices, etc	16,000
Locomotive engines, wagons and coaches	610,000
Contingencies	294,648

Plate 29 The Britannia Tubular Bridge, 1850, viewed from the Anglesey shore. The tubes were replaced by an arch structure after a fire in 1970 (*Science Museum, London*)

There are no major bridges on the route, but the excavations, embankments and tunnels were a formidable challenge to Robert Stephenson's engineering expertise. The civil engineering aspects of the line are described in Chapter 3. His heavy involvement in the construction of the London & Birmingham Railway between 1833 and 1840 was followed by further civil engineering work of a monumental scale associated with the construction of bridges in North Wales and North-East England; these bridges are the subject of Chapters 6 and 7. Returning to the London & Birmingham Railway (subsequently the London & North Western Railway after amalgamation with other railway companies), it is not widely known that the engine house at Chalk Farm in the London Borough of Camden, which now forms the principal centre of the Round House Trust, was designed by Robert Stephenson for the London & North Western Railway in 1846 (see Chapter 3). Robert Stephenson's wife Fanny died of cancer in October 1842 (see family tree) and the previous pressures of the London & Birmingham Railway, followed by those at Chester, Conwy, the Menai Strait, Newcastle and Berwick, must have contributed to his resort to heavy cigar smoking and drugs. At the height of his involvement in engineering matters in Northumberland and Wales in 1847, Stephenson became the MP for Whitby and two years later was elected a Fellow of the Royal Society and President of the Institution of Mechanical Engineers.

Further honours were awarded to Robert Stephenson in the last decade of his life. He was elected President of the Institution of Civil Engineers in 1856 and along with I. K. Brunel and Dr Livingstone, received an Honorary Doctorate of Civil Law at Oxford. Robert Stephenson was one of a small group of distinguished engineers to be elected president of both the 'Civils' and the 'Mechanicals' — the others were Thomas Hawksley (1872 C, 1876M), Sir Alexander Kennedy (1894M, 1906 C) and Sir John Aspinall (1909 M, 1918 C).

Although the crucifying pressures of previous events were not repeated in the 1850s, Stephenson's London office remained extremely active, and projects undertaken in Britain included the strengthening of a cast-iron bridge over the River Wear at Sunderland, the River Nene improvement and Liverpool waterworks. This work was not on the scale of the previous decade, but overseas, Robert Stephenson was actively engaged in a number of commissions, in particular the Victoria Tubular Bridge over the St Lawrence River, Montreal. Work overseas is the subject of Chapter 8.

In 1850, Robert Stephenson commissioned John Scott Russell

Plate 30 Thomas Telford's Menai suspension bridge taken from the road deck of the Britannia Bridge (*Frances Gibson-Smith*)

(1802–82), the naval architect, to build him a 100 ton yacht, the *Titania*. Russell was shortly to become embroiled with I. K. Brunel in the construction of the PSS *Great Eastern* (Beckett). She was launched in 1850 and Stephenson wrote (Rolt): 'she is certainly very fast, say 11 knots or 12½mph, and as a necessary consequence rather wet. I suppose it is in navigation as in mechanics, you cannot have comfort and speed at the same time . . .' This would not be a view shared by I. K. Brunel whose railways and steamships were intended to provide both. Stephenson's first major voyage was to Alexandria, but in 1852 the *Titania* was destroyed by fire while she was anchored at Cowes. Such was his enjoyment of the solitude of sea voyages that Stephenson ordered a second

Titania upon which he enjoyed many voyages, including one round Britain to visit Wylam and the Britannia Bridge. The last major voyage was a return visit to Egypt in October 1858, but his health was broken and a year later he died at his home in London.

Robert Stephenson was buried in Westminster Abbey and there is a memorial stone in the nave close to those of Thomas Telford (1757–1834) and the explorer David Livingstone (1813–73) which bears the inscription, 'Sacred to the memory of Robert Stephenson MP DCL FRS and the late President of the Institution of Civil Engineers who died 12th October AD 1859'. An application was made by Charles Manley, secretary of the Institution of Civil Engineers, to the Duke of Cambridge to permit the cortège to pass through Hyde Park en route to the abbey. The matter was immediately referred to the Queen as it was an application for which no precedent existed:

Her Majesty considers that as the late Mr Stephenson is to be buried in Westminster Abbey the acknowledgement of the high position he occupied and the worldwide reputation he had won for himself as an engineer, his funeral though strictly speaking private, as being conducted by his friends partakes of the character of a public ceremony and being anxious moreover to show that she fully shares with the public in lamenting the loss which the country has sustained by his death, she cannot hesitate for a moment in giving her entire sanction.

October is the month to visit the scene of Robert Stephenson's greatest achievement, the construction of the Britannia Bridge over the Menai Strait. The sun shining in the late afternoon opens up a vista of unique natural and man-made beauty — the autumn leaves turning from green to brown, contrasting with the majestic piers of the Britannia Bridge and, in the background, Thomas Telford's elegant suspension bridge expresses the timeless beauty of the art of engineering. One is compelled to linger in silent contemplation of Stephenson's words to Brunel when a tube of the Britannia Bridge was floated into position between the piers (see Chapter 6): 'Now, I shall go to bed.'

3

LONDON & BIRMINGHAM RAILWAY

Your scheme is preposterous in the extreme. It is of so extravagant a character, as to be positively absurd . . . Why, gentlemen, if this sort of thing is permitted to go on, you will in a few years destroy the noblesse.

(SIR ASTLEY COOPER, a landowner)

Sir Astley Cooper's comments on the proposal for constructing a railway between London and Birmingham are typical of the formidable opposition experienced by the promoters of railways from canal and coach companies and landowners. The impact of railways on long-distance stage coaches was immediate and severe — within two and a half years of the opening of the Liverpool & Manchester Railway in 1830, the number of coaches running between the two cities was reduced from twenty-nine to one. Less than three months after the opening of the London & Birmingham Railway in 1838, the number of coaches operating was reduced from twenty-two to four (H. J. Dyos and D. H. Aldroft). By 1844, the revenue of the Grand Junction Canal, the route of which is followed closely by the London & Birmingham Railway, was almost halved. The juxtaposition of road, rail and canal between London and Birmingham is one of the most interesting features of the 100mph (161kph) electric journey from the new Euston Station which covers 112 miles (180km) in 98 minutes. At the Watford Gap Service Station between junctions 16 and 17 on the M1 motorway, a distance of less than ½ mile (0.8km) separates the motorway (Sir Owen Williams, 1959), the railway (Robert Stephenson, 1838), the A5 trunk road (Thomas Telford improvements, c1815) and the Grand Junction Canal (William Jessop, 1805).

The four routes involve major civil engineering constructions and aspects of Telford's work on the A5 in North Wales are described briefly in Chapter 4. The proximity of the railway and canal routes is shown in Fig 20. The Grand Junction Canal appointed William Jessop (1744–

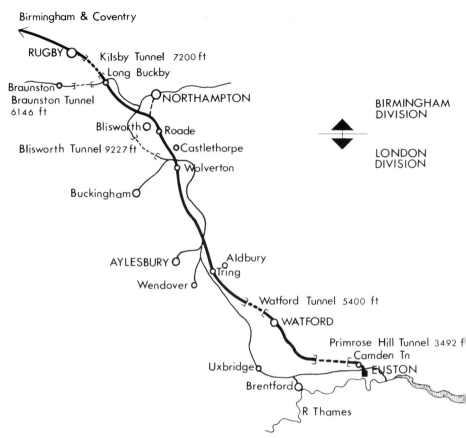

Fig 20 The route of the London & Birmingham Railway (R. Stephenson) and the Grand Junction Canal (W. Jessop)

1814) as chief engineer to the company in June 1793. In conjunction with James Barnes he was responsible for the construction of the 93½ mile (150km) route from the Oxford Canal at Braunston to the Thames at Brentford via Blisworth, Fenny Stratford (Bletchley), Tring, Hemel Hempstead, Watford, Ruislip, Southall and Hanwell (C. Hadfield and A. W. Skempton). In addition to 100 locks there were two major tunnels — at Braunston (6,146ft [1,873m]) and Blisworth (9,227ft [2,812m]).

The work, with the exception of Blisworth Tunnel, was completed in late 1800. Blisworth Tunnel was cut from nineteen vertical shafts and opened in 1805. The branch to Paddington was completed in the period 1795–1801, followed by the Regent's Canal, 1812–20, thus forming a direct link to London's docks. The Regent's Canal passes under the London & Birmingham Railway at Camden Lock.

Twenty years after the opening of the Grand Junction Canal, surveys were made for railways to connect Liverpool and Birmingham, and Birmingham and London. There was considerable rivalry over the choice of routes, and in 1829 George Stephenson instructed his assistant, Joseph Locke, to survey a route which was to connect Newton-le-Willows on the Liverpool & Manchester Railway with Warrington and then on to Birmingham via Crewe, Stafford and Wolverhampton. The Act for construction of the 80 mile (129km) Grand Junction Railway between Warrington and Birmingham received royal assent in May 1833.

Samuel Smiles gives no indication of the relationship between George Stephenson and Joseph Locke but L. T. C. Rolt puts the matter into perspective. Joseph Locke was articled to George Stephenson in 1823 and subsequently worked with him on the Liverpool & Manchester Railway. Errors in Stephenson's survey, particularly at Edgehill Tunnel, led to the directors instructing Locke to undertake another survey and report on the tunnel works. Locke prepared a report which was highly critical of the tunnel works. George Stephenson was furious, and although Joseph Locke continued for a time to work under Stephenson's direction, relations between master and pupil were strained. As we have seen in Chapter 1, George Stephenson's inability to organise major civil engineering projects became apparent during the construction of the Liverpool & Manchester Railway, but at the time of the construction of the Grand Junction Railway Locke's ability in construction management had become more widely recognised. The company opted for a compromise solution in which Locke was made responsible for the northern division and Stephenson the southern. Stephenson's administrative inefficiency soon became apparent and by the autumn of 1835 Joseph Locke had become chief engineer for the whole of the line.

Locke's route avoided as far as possible major civil engineering works, the most significant of which was the Dutton Viaduct across the valley of the River Weaver near Northwich. It consisted of twenty arches with spans of 60ft (18m) and a rise of 16ft (4.8m). The river level was 60ft (18m) below the crown of the arches. The line was opened in 1837 and the cost per mile was about one third of the London and Birmingham line, but much of this can be attributed to the absence of major civil engineering works and lower land purchase costs. The Grand Junction line was the début of Thomas Brassey (1805–70) as a railway contractor and he was later to collaborate with Peto and Betts in the construction of the Grand Trunk Railway, Canada, besides thousands of miles of lines in Europe, Australia and South America (see Chapter 8).

The most important feature of the Grand Junction Railway was the design adopted by Joseph Locke for the track. It will be recalled (see Chapter 1) that Duffy attributes the credit for the continuous development of track design to the Stephensons, but Locke's system was arguably superior. It consisted of timber sleepers spaced at 2ft 6in (0.7m) intervals with double-headed (dumb-bell) wrought-iron rail keyed into chairs with hardwood wedges (B. Morgan). It was originally intended that the rails could be turned over after one face had become worn. This was not successful and they were replaced by bull-head rail with a larger top bulge. At the time of completion of the Grand Junction Railway, Robert Stephenson was still using the fish-bellied wrought-iron rail (see Chapter 2) on the London & Birmingham Railway and stone blocks continued to be used in cuttings.

Joseph Locke went on to achieve distinction as a railway engineer, rivalling Robert Stephenson and I. K. Brunel. In addition to the Grand Junction Railway, his principal works were between the following towns and cities: London and Southampton; Sheffield and Manchester; Preston, Lancashire and Carlisle; Carlisle, Glasgow and Edinburgh; Paris, Rouen and Le Havre; Barcelona and Mattaro; and the Dutch Rhenish Railway. Distinctive features of Locke's railway works were economy, the use of masonry bridges wherever possible and the absence of tunnels — there is no tunnel between Birmingham and Glasgow. This initial economy was achieved at the expense of steep gradients which resulted in higher operating costs. In contrast, Stephenson and Brunel encountered immense problems with the construction of tunnels, the final costs greatly exceeding initial estimates (see Table 2). Following the collapse of the cast-iron bridge over the River Dee at Chester in 1847 (see Chapter 5) Joseph Locke supported Robert Stephenson at the inquest and this led to a reconciliation.

However, in the construction of the 112 mile (180km) line from London to Birmingham, Robert Stephenson was faced with construction problems which dwarfed any previous railway work, and indeed those which faced William Jessop in the construction of the Grand Junction Canal. Following the 1825 survey and further controversy over the route, George and Robert Stephenson signed an agreement in September 1830 to carry out a detailed survey (L. T. C. Rolt). George was soon to fade into the background and a second survey was undertaken by Robert Stephenson in 1831.

A year later, after severe opposition from land, coaching and canal interests, the Bill was passed by the Commons but rejected by the Lords. A third survey was carried out and, following further appeasement of the landowners by increased payments, the Bill was passed in May 1833. Five months later, Robert Stephenson was appointed the engineer to the railway. He paid far more attention to the organisation of the construction work than his father, and the line was administered by London and Birmingham divisions, the boundary being sited close to the village of Roade which is at the southern end of Blisworth cutting (see Fig 20). Each division was split into two districts: 1) Camden Town to Aldbury (a village to the east of Tring); 2) Tring to Castlethorpe (a village about 3 miles (4.8km) north of Wolverton); 3) Blisworth cutting to Kilsby Tunnel, and 4) Rugby to Birmingham.

Although there were no major bridges on the line, the final route chosen (see Plate 31) required the construction of tunnels, cuttings and embankments, examples of which are listed in Table 1.

Table 1 London & Birmingham Railway, examples of civil engineering works involved

TUNNELS		CUTTINGS		EMBANKMENTS	
Location	Length	Location	Length	Location	Length
Primrose Hill	3,492ft (1,064m)	Euston	—	North of Tring	30,000ft (9,144m)
Kensal Green	966ft (297m)	Tring	13,200ft (4,023m)	Wolverton	7,920ft (2,414m)
Watford	5,400ft (1,646m)	Blisworth	7,920ft (2,414m)		
Northchurch	1,101ft (335m)				
Linslade	852ft (260m)				
Stowe Hill	1,452ft (442m)				
Kilsby	7,200ft (2,194m)				
Carol Green	876ft (267m)				

The railway was constructed before contractors such as Thomas Brassey (1805–70) and Samuel Morton Peto (1808–89) accumulated the resources to tender for a complete division of a railway such as the Grand Trunk Railway in Canada (see Chapter 8), and thus Stephenson had no option but to sub-divide the works into thirty separate contracts (see Table 2). It is of interest to compare the contract price and revised estimate figures. There is an alarming differential for Primrose Hill and Kilsby tunnels, which reflects the difficulty of the work.

The main contractors, 30 per cent of whom fell into financial difficulties, employed an army of sub-contractors — about 20,000 men were involved in the five-year project. As a means of bolstering finances, the

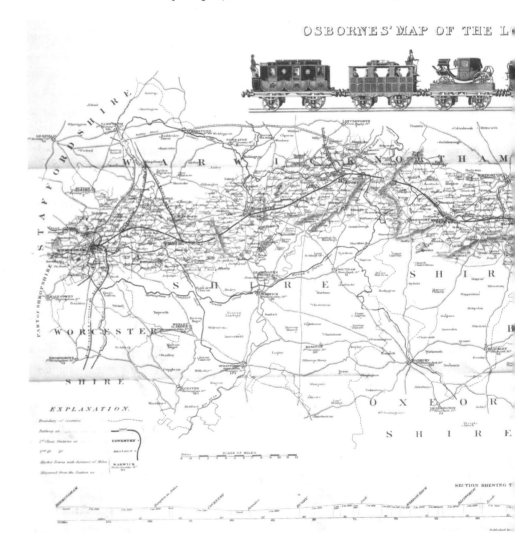

main and sub-contractors exploited the navvies (a term derived from 'navigators', men who were associated with canal construction), by opening up 'tommy' shops and lodging houses. The navvies often drank away their earnings at the tommy shops, which left them with no money for food and lodgings. The navvies were renowned for their indulgence in drunken frolics (randies), and David Brooke's *The Railway Navvy* and Terry Coleman's *The Railway Navvies* vividly describe their lives. On the credit side, the navvies' work rate was extraordinary (see p90),

Plate 31 Osborne's map of the London & Birmingham Railway with a section showing the levels and inclination of the line (*Science Museum, London*)

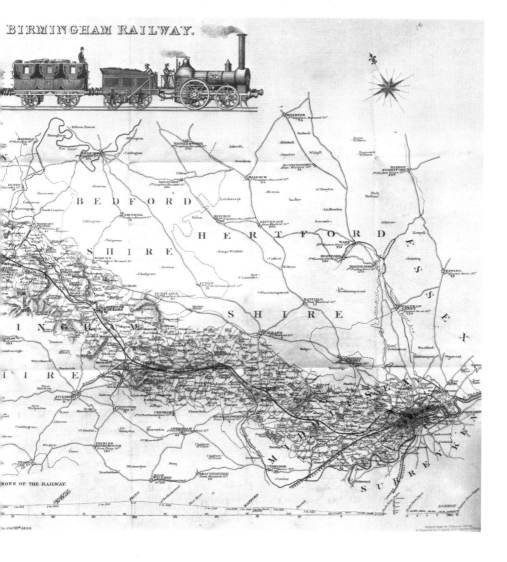

and Samuel Smiles recalls the admiration of the French onlookers for the productivity of the English navvies working on the Paris & Rouen Railway which was opened in May 1843 (contractors Mackenzie & Brassey): *'Mon Dieu; voilà ces Anglais, comme ils travaillent!'*

Table 2 The works were split into thirty contracts.

	Contract	Length Miles (km)	Contractor	Contract Price £	Revised Estimate	% Increase
1	Euston extension	1 (1.6km)	W. & L. Cubitt	76,360	91,528	19
2	Primrose Hill	5¾ (9.2km)	The company	119,981	280,014	233
3	Harrow	9½ (14.8km)	Joseph Nowell & Sons	110,227	144,574	31
4	Watford	5 (8km)	Copeland & Harding	117,000	138,219	18
5	King's Langley	2¼ (3.6km)	W. & L. Cubitt	38,900	57,386	47
6	Berkhamsted	4½ (7.2km)	W. & L. Cubitt	54,660	65,002	19
7	Aldbury	2½ (3.8km)	W. & L. Cubitt	16,694	25,134	50
8	Tring	3 (4.8km)	Assignees of Townshend	104,496	144,657	38
9	Leighton Buzzard	7½ (12km)	James Nowell	38,00	43,162	13
10	Stoke Hammond	3⅞ (6.2km)	E. W. Morris	39,303	42,345	8
11	Bletchley	3⅜ (5.4km)	John Burge	54,000	61,071	12
12	Wolverton	5 (8km)	The company	67,732	107,765	59
13	Wolverton Viaduct	⅛ (0.2km)	James Nowell	25,226	28,964	15
14	Castlethorpe	4½ (7.2km)	Craven & Sons	47,735	71,873	50
15	Blisworth	5 (8km)	The company	112,950	184,301	63
16	Baybrook	5 (8km)	John Chapman	53,400	65,013	22
17	Stowe Hill	1¼ (2km)	John Chapman	23,050	31,536	37
18	Weedon	1⅛ (1.8km)	W. & J. Simmons	26,150	31,442	20
19	Brockhall	3⅛ (5km)	J. & G. Thornton	34,157	50,583	48
20	Long Buckby	3⅝ (5.8km)	J. & G. Thornton	42,582	48,256	13
21	Kilsby	1⅜ (2.2km)	The company	98,998	291,030	294
22	Rugby	5⅛ (8.2km)	The company	59,283	93,384	57
23	Long Lawford	3¼ (5.2km)	W. & J. Simmons	20,330	25,893	27
24	Brandon	4¼ (6.8km)	The company	40,000	55,090	27
25	Avon Viaduct	1¹/₁₆ (1.7km)	S. Hemming	7,979	8,621	8
26	Coventry	7¾ (12.4km)	The company & W. &. J. Simmons	101,700	150,496	49
27	Berkswell	4½ (7.2km)	Daniel Pritchard	53,248	62,738	18
28	Yardley	7½ (12km)	Joseph Thornton	68,032	78,131	15
29	Saltley	1⅞ (3km)	James Diggle	32,878	38,707	18
30	Lea Viaduct	⅛ (0.2km)	James Nowell	13,664	15,505	14

Total 1,698,715 2,467,730

The Route

The route was staked by Robert Stephenson in the winter of 1833 and he estimated that he had walked the length of the line fifteen times by the time it was completed in 1838. One of the inns frequented by Stephenson was the Cock Inn at Stony Stratford. In January 1834, Stephenson wrote to the secretary of the Birmingham division describing the appalling weather conditions he had encountered in staking out the line. It was originally intended that the London terminus should be sited on the west side of the high road from London to Hampstead (L. T. C. Rolt), but in late 1835, parliamentary powers were obtained to extend the line to Euston Square. The contract was let to William Cubitt (1785–1861) in December 1835.

The line left Euston Square in a north-westerly direction at a gradient of 1 in 75 up to Camden Town where it crosses the Regent's Canal. Planning restrictions necessitated this steep incline which ran in a deep cutting with provision for four tracks. Four lines were proposed as it was originally intended that the Great Western and London & Birmingham railways would have a common terminus at Euston.

The Bury/Ackermann print of 1837 (Plate 32) with a view taken from under the Hampstead Road Bridge looking down towards Euston Square shows the four tracks and the massive retaining walls supporting the excavation. A line of pulleys was situated in the centre of the third and fourth tracks, to guide the cables hauling carriages up to Camden Town.

The gradient of 1 in 75 was considered to be too steep for locomotives and stationary engines with cable haulage were adopted. On a level track the force required to overcome friction is about 8lb per ton (see *Brunel's Britain*). At a gradient of 1 in 75, this increases to about 38lb. Thus the force required for a passenger train of about 60 tons (600kN) is 2,280lb (10.1kN). The average gradient on the line is about 1 in 330 (16ft [4.8m] in 1 mile [1.6km]), for which the friction reduces to less than 500lb (2.2kN) for a 60 ton train. The average gradients on the Great Western Railway were 1 in 660 and 1 in 1,320 (8ft [2.4m] and 4ft [1.2m] in 1 mile [1.6km]). Two engines were employed to haul the trains up the incline at a speed of 20mph (32kph). A different reason, however, is given in the introduction to Bourne's prints of the L & B: 'the chief cause of its [endless rope haulage] employment was the objection made by the wealthy landholders to the passage of a locomotive engine amongst the houses on this part of the line.'

Plate 32 The Bury/Ackermann print of the cutting taken from Hampstead Road Bridge looking towards Euston Square (*Science Museum, London*)

To form the cutting out of Euston, it was necessary to excavate through blue clay. The exposed clay faces were supported by immense brick retaining walls. On exposure to the atmosphere, the blue clay expands and this results in additional pressure on the walls, which failed in a number of places. The problem was overcome by constructing the walls in inverted arch form and providing a brick invert between the two walls under the track bed. In the 1830s, there was little knowledge of the properties of soils and this was the cause of most of the construction problems on subsequent sections of the route, in particular at Blisworth and Kilsby.

The original 50ft (15m) span bridge over the Regent's Canal at Camden Town is of historical significance as it was one of the earliest iron bridges to be constructed of bow-string or tied arch form — this principle was to be adopted for the High Level Bridge at Newcastle (see Chapter 7). The arches, in pairs at 3ft (0.9m) centres with a rise of 7ft

(2.1m), were tied by 3in (76mm) diameter wrought-iron rods. Plate 33 shows the current deck construction of riveted plate girders.

At Camden Town the line takes a westerly direction and passes through the 3,492ft (1,064m) long Primrose Hill Tunnel. As with the cutting to Camden, it was necessary to cut through blue clay, and again the forces exerted by the swelling owing to exposure were not anticipated. The contractor was unable to cope with the problems and the company took over with Robert Stephenson in direct control of the works. The 22ft (6.7m) wide tunnel required a brick lining three rings thick and, as can be seen from Table 2, the cost increased by more than 200 per cent of the contract price. In all, 8 million bricks were required to construct the lining and it is ventilated by an 8ft (2.4m) diameter iron shaft which rises 50ft (15m) above the tunnel.

In 1981, it was necessary to demolish an eleven-year-old block of flats and maisonettes located above the east portal in Primrose Hill Road. In addition, cracks opened in the ornate, curved, stone-faced buttress to the portals, and the brickwork inside the tunnel was showing signs of distress. The tunnel was closed for a few weeks to carry out emergency repair work and the trains were diverted through an adjacent tunnel built at a later date. The matter is still under investigation (1982).

Plate 33 The bridge over Regent's Canal at Camden Town. It was originally of bowstring girder form (*Derrick Beckett*)

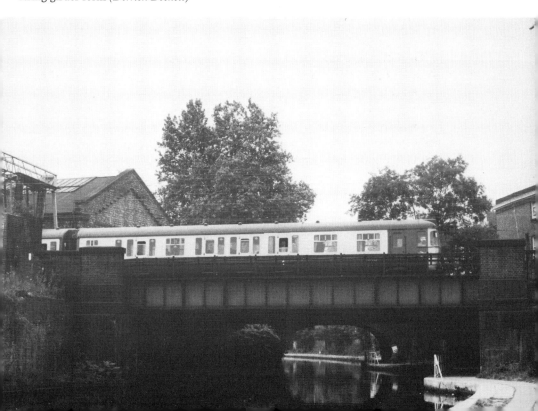

Plate 34 (*top*) The skew bridge over the A41 at Hemel Hempstead — a detail of the junction of the arch ring and abutment (*Derrick Beckett*); (*below*) Plate 35 The north portal of Northchurch Tunnel. The original Stephenson portal is on the right (*Derrick Beckett*)

Emerging from the western portal of Primrose Hill Tunnel, the line continues in a westerly direction to Kensal Green where it passes through a short tunnel. At this point, the London & Birmingham and Great Western railways are separated by less than a ¼ mile (0.4km). Kensal Green cemetery, the site of the Brunel family grave, is sandwiched between the two lines. The line then returns to a north-westerly direction and the second major tunnel is encountered at

Watford. Although Watford Tunnel is over a mile long at 5,400ft (1,645m), it was the only major work that the original contractor was able to complete without direct intervention from the company (L. T. C. Rolt). However, the problems of penetrating the chalk ridge were not as onerous as elsewhere and an invert beneath the track bed was not required. On emerging from Watford Tunnel, the canal and railway run in parallel and the line crosses the A41(T) at Hemel Hempstead on a skew bridge. The technique of construction of skew bridges has been described in Chapter 1, and Plate 34 shows the detail of the junction of the arch ring and the abutment. A few miles further on there is a short tunnel at Northchurch close to Berkhamsted (Plate 35) and the end of the first district is reached at Aldbury, near Tring (see Fig 20). The first major work on the second division (Tring to Castlethorpe) is the 13,200ft (4,023m) long cutting through the chalk ridge of Ivinghoe. The average depth of the cutting is 40ft (9.1m) and the excavation required the removal of 40 million cu ft (1,120,000m³) of material. This massive undertaking was carried out in 1837 and the excavation technique adopted is illustrated in J. C. Bourne's lithograph from his

Plate 36 J. C. Bourne's lithograph of the excavation of Tring cutting by means of horse runs (*Science Museum, London*)

Guide to the Railway, 1839 (see Plate 36); it relied almost entirely on the power of the navvy and the horse. The first stage was to contruct a narrow channel which was widened by removing the soil on horse or barrow runs. A horse at the top of the bank was harnessed to a wheelbarrow of soil by means of a rope which passed over pulleys at the top and the bottom of the post. To facilitate movement of the barrows, a wooden plankway was placed on the bank. It was a hazardous business and a faulty rope or temperamental horse would result in the navvy being precipitated to the bottom of the excavation. It is recorded that English navvies were capable of wheeling up to 450lb (2kN) of soil at a time (Smiles) and the removal of up to 20 tons (200kN) in a day. This would require ascending the wooden planking eighty times — an onerous task for the navvy and the horse.

For about ¼ mile (0.4km) of the cutting, the depth of excavation approached 60ft (18m) and forty horse runs were used to excavate the chalk and earth which was deposited in spoil banks and used for embankments north of the cutting. With slight interruptions, these embankments extend a distance of about 6 miles (9.6km) to the outskirts of Leighton Buzzard. A short distance north of Leighton Buzzard, Linslade Tunnel is approached via a 50ft (15m) deep excavation. The tunnel is constructed on a curve and the north portal is of interesting design (see Plate 37 and Gazetteer).

Plate 37 The north portal of Linslade Tunnel. The original Stephenson portal is in the centre (*Derrick Beckett*)

Plate 38 It was at Denbigh Hall that passengers had to detrain at a temporary station from April to September 1838 while the section of line on to Rugby through Kilsby Tunnel was completed. Stagecoaches provided the temporary connection. Bourne's commentary said of the bridge: 'It is stated that part of it is based on the foundations of a Roman bridge; the celebrated Watling Street of the Romans having occupied the site and line of the present Great North Road. The whole length of the bridge is 200 feet and the height from the road to the soffit of the arch is twenty feet' (*Locomotive & General Railway Photographs*); (*below*) Plate 39 The deck structure of the cast-iron bridge over the A5 at Denbigh Hall near Bletchley (*Derrick Beckett*)

About 48 miles (77km) from London, the line crosses the A5, originally the London and Holyhead turnpike road, via Denbigh Hall
Bridge (Plate 38). Although no longer in use, the structure remains and
Plate 39 shows the cast-iron deck structures and stone piers. The 34ft
(10m) span cast-iron beams are placed at right angles to the abutments
and as the line crosses the bridge at a skew, it was necessary to make the
abutments 200ft (61m) long. An alternative would have been to construct narrow abutments with the cast-iron girders placed on the skew
with the length increased to 80ft (24m). The unreliability of cast iron in
beam form is described elsewhere, together with Stephenson's use of
wrought-iron ties to offset cast-iron's deficiencies. At 80ft (24m) span, a
single casting would not have been possible.

The highest embankment on the line is reached at Wolverton, about
52 miles (84km) from London and its average height is 48ft (14.6m).
Over 13 million cu ft (364,000m³) of material was required for the 1½
mile (2.4km) length. Again, lack of knowledge of soil mechanics resulted in slip and settlement problems. There is a gap in the embankment where the line crosses the River Ouse. The river is crossed by a
viaduct which has six major semi-elliptical arches of 60ft (18m) span
(see Plate 40). At each end there are two massive pilasters followed by
three smaller arches which pierce the retaining walls built in the shape
of the embankment. A close-up of one of the piers (Plate 41) shows the
demarcation line between the original and new structure, which was required when the line was quadrupled. Surprisingly, the final cost of
£28,000 was only 15 per cent greater than the contract price (Table 2).
The second division of the line terminated at Castlethorpe, a short distance to the north of Wolverton embankment.

The third district ran from Blisworth, situated at the northern end of
Jessop's canal tunnel, to Roade at the southern end of Stephenson's
7,920ft (2,414m) long cutting. Once again, after a year and a half of
strenuous effort the contractor was defeated and Robert Stephenson
took over. Excavation down to 65ft (20m) deep in places required the
removal of 27 million cu ft (765,000m³) of earth, stiff clay and rock. The
final cost reached almost three times the contract price and the primary
cause was the differing properties of the soil strata. Herculean efforts
were required from the engineer and navvies to achieve the eventual
completion of the works. About one-third of the total excavation was in
rock which was removed by blasting. Holes 1in (25mm) in diameter
were drilled in the rock to a depth governed by the thickness of the bed.
A fuse was inserted and gunpowder packed round it with a cover of

Plate 40 The Wolverton viaduct over the River Ouse with six main spans of 60ft (18m) (*Derrick Beckett*)

Plate 41 A close-up of one of the piers showing the demarcation line between the original arch and the subsequent widening to accommodate an additional double line (*Derrick Beckett*)

Plate 42 Roade cutting looking north in 1937 with an up train on the Northampton loop
(*Locomotive & General Railway Photographs*)

Plate 43 A view looking south towards Roade taken from a bridge over the north end of
the cutting, showing the massive retaining walls. The main line is on the right (*Derrick
Beckett*)

pounded brick. Three thousand barrels of gunpowder were used to blast the rock and a locomotive was provided at each end of the cutting to facilitate removal of the excavated material.

The rock did not extend to the full depth of the required level of excavation, and clay followed by water-filled shale were encountered. Removal of the water required the installation of two steam engines to work the pumps. The excavation below the rock was not inherently stable and thus massive retaining walls were required, with inverts constructed beneath the tracks to achieve stability. On completion of the retaining walls, a culvert 3ft 6in (1m) high x 3ft (0.9m) wide was formed to collect water flowing from the strata behind, thus preventing the build-up of water pressure. Openings were also provided in the retaining walls and the water collected in the side drains to the railway. The photograph taken from a bridge at the north end of the cutting (Plate 43) at the junction with the Northampton loop (see Gazetteer), emphasises the scale of the works. The bridge itself naturally had to be widened to accommodate the Northampton loop (Plate 44).

North of Blisworth, the railway and canal again run in parallel and the line passes through the sixth tunnel at Stowe Hill. The juxtaposition of canal, road and railway continues for a further 9 miles (15km) and at

Plate 44 The bridge over the north end of the cutting. The original Stephenson arch is on the right *(Derrick Beckett)*

Plate 45 J. C. Bourne's lithograph conveys the frenzied activity required to lower the water level (*Science Museum, London*)

Kilsby ridge Robert Stephenson was faced with the last and most hazardous section of the line to be completed, the 7,200ft (2,194m) long tunnel at Kilsby. The tunnel runs at an average depth of about 160ft (49m) below the surface of a ridge of limestone (oolite) which is also pierced by canal tunnels at Braunston and Crick. The first stage of the project was to sink trial shafts to ascertain the nature of the soil strata, but unfortunately these shafts did not reveal the extent of a mass of unstable sand saturated with water (quicksand).

Robert Stephenson was aware of the presence of quicksands but underestimated its effect on the cost and construction time for the tunnel. The contract was let to James Nowell and it was proposed to sink sixteen shafts from which headings would be driven towards each other. In the gap between two shafts which had been sunk near the south end of the tunnel, quicksand was encountered, causing the roof of the tunnel to collapse and works to be flooded. There were similar problems at other shafts. The strain of the construction problems was too much for the contractor; he was taken ill and died shortly after. A further attempt to drain off the water was attempted by excavating a secondary tunnel parallel to the main tunnel into which it was hoped to collect the water from the main tunnel. This was not successful as it was soon blocked by sand.

Robert Stephenson consulted his father who was then living at Alton Grange on the Snibston Estate, near Ashby de la Zouch. George Stephenson moved to Alton Grange from Liverpool in 1831 to supervise coal-mining interests and he anticipated that use could be made of the railway under construction close by to transport the coal to Leicester. The inevitable solution was to rely on the power of the steam engine, and thirteen pumping engines were placed along the line of the tunnel. Pumping operations were continued for a period of nineteen months with extraction rates averaging 2,000gal (9,092 litres) per minute.

J. C. Bourne's lithograph of the Kilsby Tunnel under construction, showing steam-powered pumps and horse gins (Plate 45) gives a dramatic impression of the scale of the operations involved. Eventually it was possible to suck the water back from the line of the excavation, enabling the tunnel to be lined to a thickness of 27in (70cm), requiring 30 million engineering bricks. The work-force rose to 1,300 men and 200 horses. The majority of the men lived in crude self-made, turf-roofed huts and the residents of Kilsby endured numerous randies which took place on Kilsby Green. In December 1837, the works were nearing completion and George Stephenson attended a celebration

Plate 46 Kilsby Tunnel: J. C. Bourne's lithograph of the 60ft (18m) diameter, 130ft (40m) deep ventilation shaft *(Science Museum, London)*

dinner at the Dun Cow Inn, Dunchurch, a village south of Rugby. Robert left the table at 2.00 am, George at 4.00 am, and drinking continued until 8.00 am.

The landscape over the line of the tunnel is dominated by two massive ventilation shafts (Plate 46). The first was commenced in May 1836 and completed in about twelve months. The shaft is 60ft (18m) in diameter,

99

132ft (40m) deep and the brick walls are 3ft (0.9m) thick. The second shaft is of similar construction but 30ft (9m) shallower. They were built from the top downwards by excavating a small portion of the wall at a time from 6ft (1.8m) to 12ft (3.6m) in length and 10ft (3m) deep. Bourne's lithograph (Plate 46) shows a completed ventilation shaft — note the rails supported on stone blocks. The south portal (Plate 47) is the more impressive of the two, but its scale, in contrast to the ventilation shafts, is not indicative of the magnitude of the civil engineering works involved.

On leaving Kilsby Tunnel, the line passes through Rugby, 82 miles (132km) from London. With the exception of Beechwood Tunnel at Carol Green to the west of Coventry, 876ft (267m) long, and the 10-arch viaduct over Lawley Street in Birmingham, 711ft (216m) long, the scale of work on the remaining 30 miles (48km) from Rugby to Birmingham is modest compared with that at Kilsby, Blisworth and Tring.

The buildings constructed at Curzon Street, Birmingham, were most impressive and included a goods station, passenger station, warehouses, offices and an engine house (J. C. Jeafferson). The offices, including the directors' boardroom, were contained in a building hav-

Plate 47 The south portal of Kilsby Tunnel (*Derrick Beckett*)

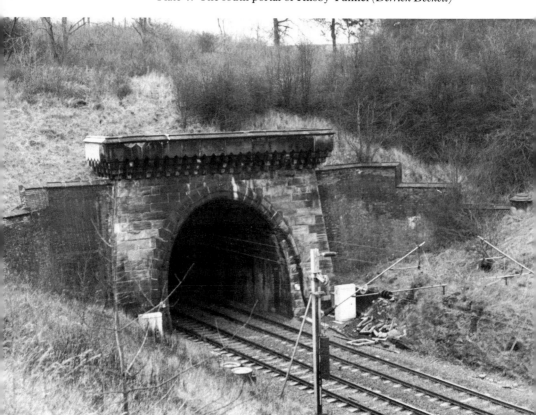

Plate 48 Curzon Street Station, Birmingham, in 1937. Designed by Philip Hardwick, who was also responsible for Euston, the station was built by Grissell & Peto at a cost of £26,000. The main building, with a portico of four Ionic columns in front and four three-quarter columns in the rear, contained a refreshment room, directors' apartment, and secretaries'and engineers' offices (*Locomotive & General Railway Photographs*)

ing a portico with Ionic columns designed by P. Hardwick (see p104). The contractors were Messrs Grissell & Peto and the building costs were £26,000. The station entrance was to one side of the building and the booking offices were contained in a long building having a colonnade in front. The six lines of track were covered by a roof 217ft (66m) long, 113ft (34m) wide, which was considered to be one of the finest in the world. The tied wrought-iron rafters were supported by a series of open ornamented cast-iron girders which in turn were carried on three rows of cast-iron columns. The total roof weight, including timber planking and slates, was estimated to be 326 tons (3,260kN).

The locomotives were housed in a sixteen-sided building which could accommodate sixteen locomotives and tenders or thirty-two engines alone. Access to the engines for cleaning and maintenance work was via

3ft (1m) deep pits under each of the tracks. According to Jeafferson, the water laid on by the Birmingham Water Company was at such great pressure that it caused the death of a boy who was attempting to remove a wooden plug driven into one of the waterways: 'it flew out like a shot beating him on the skull and killing him on the spot'.

Robert Stephenson hoped to have the line operational by the end of January 1838, but it was not officially opened for two-line running until September 1838. In the period from January to September 1838, a train service ran between London and a temporary terminus at Denbigh Hall Inn situated north of Bletchley where the A5 (Watling Street) is crossed by the railway. A coach service operated between Denbigh Hall and Rugby via Towcester and Dunchurch. The journey continued by train between Rugby and Birmingham which formed division four of the line. The actual cost of the line was £5.5 million, well over twice the estimated cost of £2.4 million.

Robert Stephenson's involvement in the Forth Street works at Newcastle prevented Robert Stephenson & Co from supplying locomotives due to accusations of monopoly. For the period 1837–47, Edward Bury (1794–1858), who was the company's locomotive superintendent at Wolverton, was responsible for supplying and maintaining the locomotives. It was not until 1844 that sufficient power had been developed to enable rope haulage to be abandoned on the incline between Euston and Camden Town. Stephenson's responsibility for the construction of the London & Birmingham Railway did not end on the September 1838 opening date as the time-dependent properties of soil, combined with the results of inadequate understanding of the need for thorough compaction of soil on embankments, necessitated constant inspection of the line, speed restrictions and frequent packing of the track. However, track maintenance has always been a major problem for British Rail. Line replacement now costs about £300,000 per mile (1.6km) and speed restrictions have had to be imposed on a number of sections of the network, due to inadequate investment, to ensure adequate safety margins.

An early major addition to the railway was the engine shed designed by Robert Stephenson at Chalk Farm. The following account of the Round House is based on abstracts from the *Illustrated London News* (4 December 1847) and *The Builder* (1847) which were included in the first report of the Round House Trust, December 1965 to March 1971. The objects of the trust include the encouragement of all the arts, including those of drama, mime, dancing, singing and music. The photograph in

Plate 49 The internal structure of the Round House. The walls are built on a 160ft (49m) diameter with twenty-four cast-iron internal columns on an 80ft (24m) diameter

Plate 50 The Round House by John Piper

Plate 51 is taken from the west side of the building and the internal structural form is shown in Plate 49.

This building is a circular form, 160 feet in diameter in the clear of the walls. The roof is supported on 24 columns at equal distances, and forms a circle 40 feet in diameter [they mean radius] from the centre of the building.

The columns are 21 feet nine inches high. On top of these columns are 24 cast iron girders, running in a straight line between each column and connected to each column with bolts. These girders are formed into an arch, being two feet nine deep; the top flange is moulded, and the spandrils perforated directly over the columns; and connected with them are an equal number of standards, 30 feet 3 inches in height, from the top of the girders. At the top they are flanged each way, to receive the purlins and member rafters, 24 of which run up the lantern-light, and 12 finish on the purlins, at the top of the standards.

The lantern-light stands 4 feet 3 inches from the roof and is formed at the same inclination with the roof, with wood louvres at the sides, and cast iron sash-bars at the top, and covered with rough plate glass; at the top is a piece of cast iron, 2 feet 6 inches in diameter, into which the tops of the sash bars are fastened; at the apex is a large wooden ball, covered with 10lbs of lead.

The height from the line of rails to the tension-rod is 25 feet. The member rafters drop on a cast iron shoe and standards, and are secured with screws. The top part of the principals and lantern-light are supported by cast iron brackets, spreading from the bottom of the standards and secured to the principals within 9 feet of the curb lantern. From the line of rails to the top of concrete is 2 feet 6 inches, with a bed of concrete 2 feet 6 inches deep, making a total from the bottom of concrete to the top of ball of 93 feet 6 inches.

The foundation of the building is immensely strong having 24 transverse walls, 2½ bricks thick. These walls run in pairs, at parallel widths, from the outside walls, within 25 feet 9 inches of the centre, which form the bed for the rails to lay on to receive the engines; and the walls are connected by an invert at the bottom, a semi-arch at the top which forms the bottom of the ash-pits.

The building had one entrance for the engines on the west side and there were two smaller doorways. A turntable 36ft (11m) in diameter was placed in the centre of the building to enable the engines to be turned into one of the twenty-three radiating lines. Fifteen years after its completion, the engine house was converted into a goods shed as the engines and tenders became too long for the turntable and bays. In 1869, the building was leased to W. & A. Gilbey Ltd as a liquor store.*

The modest train sheds at Euston were fronted by a monumental entrance designed by Philip Hardwick (1792–1870). The Doric portico

*Unfortunately, financial difficulties have recently (March 1983) forced the Round House Theatre to close and discussions are underway as to its future as a theatre or otherwise. Let us hope that those involved will appreciate the historical significance of this unique building.

Plate 51 The Round House Theatre at Chalk Farm which closed in March 1983 owing to financial difficulties (*Derrick Beckett*)

forming the main carriage entrance to Euston Station was one of the most imposing examples of nineteenth-century London architecture, but unfortunately it was demolished, despite numerous protests, to make way for the new Euston Station which was opened by Queen Elizabeth in 1968. In addition to the portico, Philip Hardwick and his son Philip C. Hardwick (1822–92) designed possibly the most elegant waiting hall in London's historic railway stations — the Great Hall at Euston. It was opened in May 1849 and was 126ft (38m) long, 61ft (18m) wide and 64ft (19m) high. Amongst the architectural features were the clerestory windows, coffered ceiling and double staircase. The central feature of the hall was a statue of George Stephenson. Regrettably, the Great Hall suffered the same fate as the portico, but the statue of George Stephenson is now safely installed at the National Railway Museum, York. In contrast to the magnificent nineteenth-century train sheds at St Pancras and Paddington, the architectural poverty of Euston Station is such that there is no encouragement to linger in the vast entrance hall, but for the businessman with a tight one-day schedule in Milton Keynes, Birmingham, Manchester or Liverpool, it works well enough. Birmingham New Street Station, the replacement for Curzon

Street, has also been rebuilt, and in recent years two new major stations have been opened — Birmingham International and Milton Keynes.

Birmingham International Station provides direct access to the National Exhibition Centre and an elevated monorail (MAGLEV) currently under construction will link the new station with the airport. The station at Milton Keynes completes the city's rail, road and bus transportation systems.

Of all the nineteenth- and twentieth-century constructions on the London & Birmingham Railway the most symbolic are the two castellated towers of the 60ft (18m) diameter, 120ft (36m) deep ventilation shafts of Kilsby Tunnel which can be seen from the A5 as it crosses the limestone ridge. They are a permanent reminder of the herculean task which faced Robert Stephenson and his work-force of 20,000 men between 1833 and 1838.

Plate 52 The statue of George Stephenson at the National Railway Museum, York, was originally the central feature of the Great Hall at Euston Station (*Frances Gibson-Smith*)

4

CHESTER & HOLYHEAD RAILWAY

The simple fact that in a heavy storm the force of impact of the waves is from one and a half to two tons per square foot, must necessarily dictate the greatest possible caution in approaching so formidable an element.

(ROBERT STEPHENSON)

Improvement in communications by road, rail and sea between London and Dublin via Bangor and Holyhead, and also along the North Wales coast to link Bangor and Chester to facilitate travel between Ireland and the North of England has, over the past 150 years, presented a formidable challenge to the ingenuity of civil engineers. The variable topography and· great natural beauty of Snowdonia and the Conwy Valley has always required careful assessment of the choice of route. This is even more important today: the planners of the A55 trunk road, now under construction between St Asaph and Aber via Colwyn Bay, Conwy and Penmaenmawr, are required to take account of greater public interest in route evaluation, traffic patterns, economic and environmental considerations and disturbance to existing urban areas. The effect of a new road on monuments, buildings and bridges of historical and architectural interest requires detailed consideration, and it is of interest to note that Robert Stephenson was able to take his railway through the town walls of Conwy. It is difficult to imagine that any proposal to take a dual carriageway through the town walls of Conwy would now gain public acceptance.

Telford's Routes

Telford surveyed routes for a mail-coach road between London and Holyhead (260 miles [418km]) and from Chester to Bangor (60 miles [96km]) some thirty-five years prior to commencement of work on the Chester & Holyhead Railway. The London and Holyhead road is now classified as the A5 and the section between Shrewsbury and Bangor is an outstanding example of highway engineering in terms of alignment and gradient. The gradient does not exceed 1 in 20 and there are some excellent examples of Telford's bridge-building skills, including the Waterloo Bridge at Betws-y-Coed, a cast-iron arch opened in 1816 and the Menai Suspension Bridge opened in 1826 (see Chapter 6). The Menai Bridge offers an excellent view of the Britannia Bridge, which is a short distance westward. In 1981 an exhibition celebrating the history of the Menai bridges (Pontydd Menai), presented by the Gwynedd Archives Services in Association with the Welsh Arts Council, was held at the Science Museum, London. The exhibition included some outstanding photographs and drawings and an excellent illustrated booklet from which the following reference to the Menai Suspension Bridge is taken:

This immense work, which in all its parts is regulated by the principle of utility, is totally deficient in all the charms of beauty. It cuts the landscape like a black uniform line, concave on one side, and perfectly horizontal on the other and when viewed closely, the columns by which the bridge is supported, are wholly destitute of every description of architectural or sculptural ornament . . . Other bridges, with their various arches and ornamental buttresses, may, and frequently do present objects of great beauty to the eye. This, however, is, and must always remain, a great mathematical figure.

(*The King of Saxony's Journey thro' England and Scotland* by his physician Dr C. G. Carus, 1844).

The photograph taken from the Anglesey approaches to the Britannia Bridge demonstrates Dr Carus's lack of appreciation of the art of engineering which was better understood by John Smith in his *Guide to Snowdonia*: 'there is so much magnificence, beauty and elegance in this grand work of art, that it harmonises and accords perfectly with the natural scenery around, and though itself an object of admiration, still in connexion it heightens the effect of general view' (*Wanderings through North Wales*, Thomas Roscoe, 1836). Telford's improvements to the North Wales coast road involved the construction of a suspension bridge over the Conwy estuary, which was completed in 1826. Its towers were built to harmonise with those of Conwy Castle. Twenty-two years later Robert Stephenson's tubular railway bridge was completed, again with abutments designed to complement the architecture of the castle.

The A55 is now carried by an arched road bridge opened in 1959. The Telford road and Stephenson's railway run almost in parallel between Conwy and Bangor, but a number of improvements to the road have been required as the result of rock falls. At Paenmaenbach Point, a

Plate 53 An up express leaving the Conwy Tubular Bridge behind a 'Problem' class 2–2–2 and a 4–4–0 compound in the late nineteenth century. The first stone was laid on 12 May 1846 and Robert Stephenson drove the first train over the bridge on 18 April 1848. The masonry was designed by Francis Thompson (architect to the North Midland Railway) to harmonise with the adjacent late thirteenth-century castle, designed by Master James of St George (*Locomotive & General Railway Photographs*)

Plate 54 Looking towards Penmaenbach Point; the railway is behind the sea wall and Telford's original road follows the cliff edge round the point (*Frances Gibson-Smith*)

short distance west of Conwy, the original road follows the cliff edge round the point and in 1932 the road was diverted through a tunnel (Plate 54).

Stephenson's Route

Prior to Telford's improvements, the A5 was one of the worst roads in Britain and travelling conditions were appalling. Coaches often took five hours to cover 14 miles (22km) and at best, the maximum speed was 10mph (16kph). By 1843, average train speeds, exclusive of stoppages, were about 30mph (48kph). With the opening of the Britannia Bridge in 1850, the 84½ mile (136km) train journey from Chester to Holyhead took 2 hours 40 minutes (G. Drysdale Dempsey) with an average speed of about 32mph (51kph). In 1983 the Chester–Llandudno–Holyhead train service has a fastest time of 1 hour 31 minutes with an average speed of about 56mph (74kph) — not a vast improvement in a period of 132 years. The intermediate stations on the route (1850 and 1982) are shown in the table below and Llanfairpwll station formerly had the longest name in the world: LLANFAIRPWLLGWYNGYLLGOGERYCAWYRNDROBWLL LLAN YSILIOGOGOGOCH. (translation: St Mary's Church in the white hazel hollow near to the rapid whirlpool and St Tysilios Church by the red cave).

Stations 1850	Stations 1982	Miles (km) from Chester
Chester	●	—
Queensferry		7 (11.2km)
Flint	●	12½ (20.1km)
Bagilt		14½ (23.3km)
Holywell		16¾ (26.9km)
Mostyn		20 (32.1km)
Prestatyn	●	26¼ (42.2km)
Rhyl	●	30 (48.2km)
Abergele	●	34¼ (55.1km)
Colwyn	●	40¼ (64.7km)
Conway		45¼ (105km)
Aber		54¼ (87.7km)
Bangor	●	59³/₁₀ (95.4km)
Llanfairpwll	●	63½ (102km)
Gaerwen		66½ (107km)
Bodorgan	●	72½ (116.6km)
Ty Croes	●	75½ (121.5km)
Valley	●	81 (130.3km)
Holyhead	●	84½ (135.9km)

Plate 55 Penmaenmawr Viaduct and Tunnel with Telford's Holyhead road above
(*Science Museum, London*)

The Act for the construction of the Chester & Holyhead Railway was given royal assent on 4 July 1844 and Robert Stephenson was appointed engineer. After crossing the River Dee at Chester, the scene of the collapse of Stephenson's cast-iron composite girders (see Chapter 5), the line follows the course of the river to the estuary and then the coastline for practically the whole of the distance between the Dee estuary and Holyhead.

The view out to the sea on the first stage of the journey through Flint, Prestatyn and Rhyl is somewhat marred by a galaxy of caravans and beach huts and dilapidated amusement areas. It is unfortunate that the degree of meticulous attention paid to the effect of the new A55 trunk road on the environment does not appear to be given to the siting of caravan parks. At Colwyn Bay there is an interesting juxtaposition of Stephenson's railway, Telford's road and the A55 trunk road currently under construction. After passing through Llandudno Junction the line crosses the River Conwy estuary via the tubular bridge (for detailed description see Chapter 6), skirts the castle walls on the landward side and pierces the town wall at the site of the old Conway Station. The station is now used as an information centre. The tubular bridge is undergoing extensive maintenance, including repairs to the roof and re-painting. The colour scheme is being changed from a dullish grey to a more attractive brown.

On leaving Conwy, the Penmaenbach headland is negotiated by a 2,000ft (610m) long tunnel and the line is then carried on a massive sea wall beneath the steep slope of Penmaenmawr. Stephenson experienced great difficulties in constructing the sea walls at Penmaenmawr and an account by Henry Swinburne of their construction was given in the March 1851 proceedings of the Institution of Civil Engineers. Work on the main sea walls commenced in the spring of 1846 and a profile of the wall with an ashlar facing set in cement and continued to 6ft (1.8m) above high-water spring tides is shown in Fig 21. The shingle between the wall and the part of the cliff was piled against the back of the wall to support it and at the same time relieve pressure from the embankment by reversing the slope of its base. On 26 October 1846 a gale destroyed the central portion of the main sea wall with a tide of 17ft (5m). The cause of the failure was not the force of the waves but the penetration of water washing away the rubble backing to the ashlar facing (Fig 22).

It was necessary to condemn about 600ft (183m) of the wall and an open viaduct was substituted (see Plate 55). The cofferdams for the foundations to the piers were commenced in May 1847. The 7ft (2m) thick piers, at a spacing of 42ft (13m), were taken up to 41ft (12m) above foundation level (16ft [5m] above Trinity high-water level). This section of the line was opened for traffic in May 1848 and Plate 55 depicts the scene in 1849. Telford's Holyhead road was cut out of the rock about 250ft (76m) above the railway level. Penmaenbach headland can be seen in the background.

The remaining portions of the wall were constructed in the form shown in Fig 23 and founded at a greater depth than the earlier sections to allow for subsidence of the beach. In order to protect the foundations to the older sections of the wall, a breakwater and terrace were formed. Timber piles (Fig 24) were driven in zig-zag rows a clear distance of 2ft (0.6m) apart. Bays of five piles were formed and the piles were backed with several tiers of 3in (76mm) thick planks. An artificial beach was formed between piles and the sea wall. As the word breakwater implies, its purpose was to break up the waves and prevent water flowing over the parapet of the sea wall, but it was found that in lowering the beach in front of the breakwater, the action of the surf was amplified. It was considered necessary to form a steep apron in front of the piles, but it was not possible to prevent an oblique surf in March 1848 sweeping away the shingle between the piles and the sea wall. The consulting engineers for the A55 coast road, R. Travers Morgan & Partners, have taken the precaution of building a trial embankment where the road at Colwyn Bay crosses the railway and runs along the foreshore. The foreshore area is subject to landslips and the subsoil profile is complex and variable. Movement has been continuously monitored and the embankment has been designed to form a stabilising load to prevent slips. It is faced with sea defences to protect it against erosion. To return to the railway, Stephenson arrived at the conclusion that in railway works engineers should endeavour as far as possible to avoid the necessity of contending with the sea (Smiles).

One further problem remained and that was the construction of the Britannia Tubular Bridge over the Menai Strait about 1 mile (1.6km) east of Telford's suspension bridge. A detailed description of the construction of this bridge is given in Chapter 6 and a structural assessment is included in an Appendix. It is now possible to cross the reconstructed Britannia Bridge by road or rail. A section of the original tube has been retained and is mounted on a plinth located on the embankment leading down to the Caernarvon shore on the western side of the bridge. The wrought-iron plates are in excellent condition and their thinness is immediately apparent. An appreciation of the scale of the structure can be

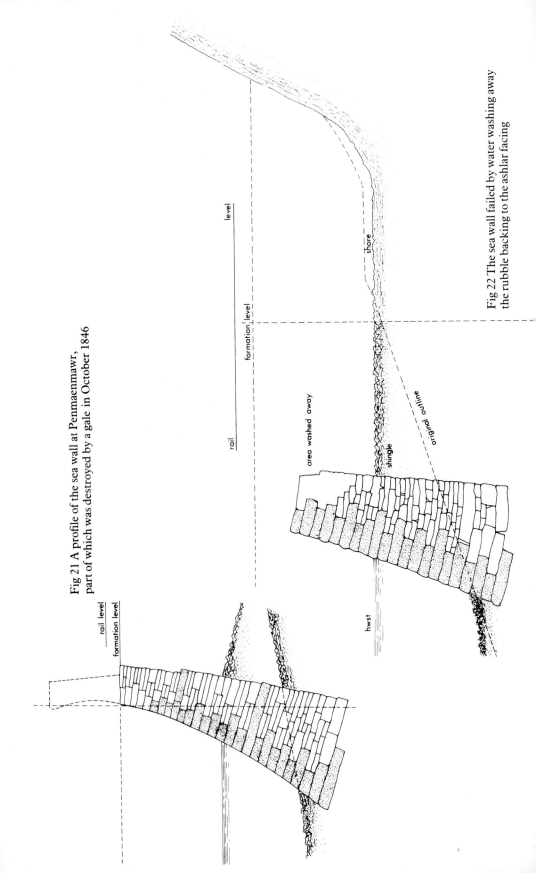

Fig 21 A profile of the sea wall at Penmaenmawr, part of which was destroyed by a gale in October 1846

Fig 22 The sea wall failed by water washing away the rubble backing to the ashlar facing

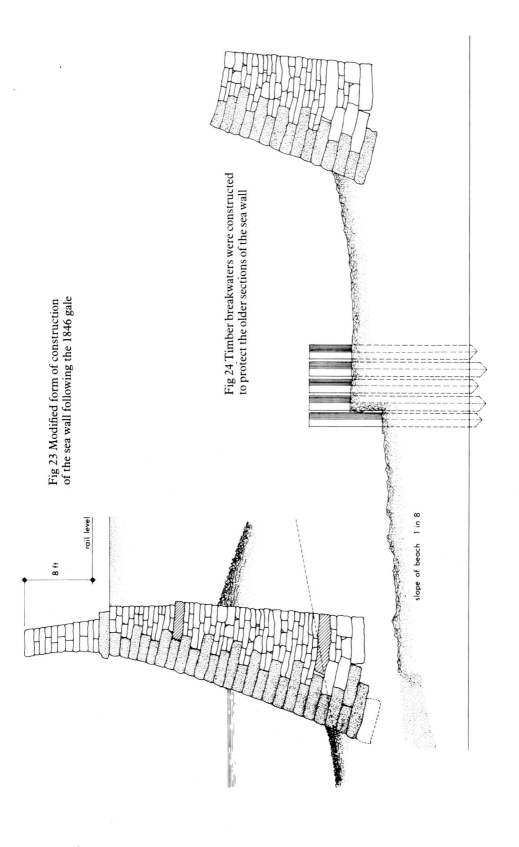

Fig 23 Modified form of construction
of the sea wall following the 1846 gale

Fig 24 Timber breakwaters were constructed
to protect the older sections of the sea wall

8 ft

rail level

slope of beach   1 in 8

gained by standing inside it. Fortunately, it was possible to utilise the existing piers and the Anglesey marble (carboniferous limestone) has weathered well. The approaches to the bridge on each side are ornamented by massive statues of lions in Egyptian style. They consist of eleven pieces of limestone and weigh about 30 tons (Clark). The original Britannia Bridge has been referred to as 'that 'ere great, long, ugly iron thing', but its immense physical presence and technical merit cannot be disputed.

The fire of 23-5 May 1970 (see p147) caused such severe damage to the Britannia tubes that they were irreparable. Had the fire not occurred, the tubes would be carrying the trains today, and it is a tribute to the engineering judgement of Robert Stephenson that his major bridges crossing the Menai Strait and the rivers Conwy, Tyne and Tweed have met the requirements of the British Standard Code of Practice for bridges (BS 5400: 1978). The following extract is taken from Part 1.

A design life of 120 years has been assumed throughout BS 5400 (unless otherwise stated). The assumption of a design life does not necessarily mean that the structure will no longer be fit for its purpose at the end of that period, or that it will continue for that length of time without adequate and regular inspection and maintenance. It is to be emphasised that bridges like most modern structures, require regular inspection and, when necessary, repair under competent direction . . .

It was stated previously that the Conwy tubes are currently undergoing maintenance.

The Chester & Holyhead Railway is possibly rivalled in terms of hazardous construction problems and scenic interest by Brunel's route for the South Devon Railway between Exeter and Plymouth. It was built during a similar time-scale and the section between Starcross and Teignmouth required the construction of a sea wall and a number of tunnels. The line reached Plymouth in 1848, but the crossing of the River Tamar via the Royal Albert Bridge at Saltash (see p131) was not completed until ten years later. This bridge has also met the British Standard's requirement of a design life of 120 years with reasonable maintenance.

It is of interest to speculate on how Robert Stephenson, and even more so his father, would have reacted to the planning needed to divert the Chester & Holyhead Railway at Colwyn Bay. From Marine Road to Station Road, which is about half-way between the town centre and the River Conwy estuary, the railway is being diverted northwards and the new road built on the existing railway formation. In a few years time there will be a unique combination of road and rail routes at Penmaen-bach headland (see p110). A new tunnel is to be constructed inland of the railway tunnel to provide a new carriageway for the westbound traffic on the A55 North Wales coast road. Construction is expected to start in 1984 and will take about two and a half years. Drill and blast methods will be required to drive the tunnel and care will need to be taken to control blast-induced vibrations as the generally unlined railway tunnel, completed c1848, is only about 200ft (61m) away from the new tunnel. Eastbound traffic will continue to use the existing tunnel (1932), which is to the north of the rail tunnel, but the long-term intention is to provide a second tunnel for eastbound traffic. Part of the old Telford road (c1820), which skirts the edge of the headland, still remains.

5

COLLAPSE OF THE BRIDGE
OVER THE RIVER DEE

*Cast iron girder bridges are always giving trouble — from such cases as
the Chester Bridge and our own Great Western road bridge at Hanwell
which, since 1838 has always been under repair and has cost its first cost
three times over down to petty little ones, which, either in frosty weather
or from other causes, are frequently failing. I never use cast iron if I can
help it.*

(I. K. BRUNEL)

The Chester Bridge referred to by Brunel in his letter of 18 April 1849 to
the directors of the Great Western Railway collapsed on 24 May 1847. It
was designed by Robert Stephenson to carry the Chester and Holyhead
and Chester and Shrewsbury lines over the River Dee. Fifteen years
earlier, Marc Brunel advised on the design of a 200ft (61m) span
masonry arch road bridge crossing the River Dee at Chester (Grosvenor
Bridge). For the railway, Stephenson planned to construct a five-span
arch bridge in brick, but poor ground conditions necessitated a change
in the design. There were a number of options open to Stephenson and
the lightest construction would have been to build a timber viaduct of
the form developed by I. K. Brunel for the line west of Exeter. This was
possibly rejected on the grounds of lack of rigidity and durability. This
left iron as the final choice of material and the forms of iron in use in the
1840s were wrought iron and cast iron. Both were obtained from iron
ore in which the iron is in chemical combination with other materials.
These are partially removed by the process of smelting in a blast
furnace.

In 1709 at Coalbrookdale in Shropshire, Abraham Darby 1 (1677–
1711) first successfully smelted iron ore using coke as a fuel to replace
charcoal, and by the mid-eighteenth century this process was widely
used. The iron after smelting is known as pig iron, and cast iron is
manufactured from suitable pig iron by smelting and casting the molten

120

metal directly into moulds. Cast iron is too brittle to be shaped by rolling or hammering. The first bridge to be constructed in cast iron was the iron bridge over the River Severn at Coalbrookdale which forms the centre-piece of the Ironbridge Gorge Museum. The bridge was built by the ironmaster Abraham Darby III (1750–91). The arch form is more appropriate for cast iron than a beam system since cast iron is unreliable in tension, that is, extension of the material fibres. In assessing the strength of cast-iron members, London County Council, in 1909, recommended the following values:

tension $\quad$ = $\quad 1\frac{1}{2}$ tons/in² (23.2 N/mm²)
compression $\quad$ = $\quad$ 8 tons/in² (123.6 N/mm²)

William Fairbairn and Eaton Hodgkinson conducted a series of tests to devise the most appropriate section for a cast-iron beam. It is apparent that a beam resting between supports will develop tension in the bottom fibres and compression in the top fibres. For a material that is weak in tension, a greater proportion of the total material in a given cross-section should be concentrated in the bottom section and thus the inverted T-section (Fig 25) was considered to be the optimum form. From tests on models up to 10ft (3m) span, Hodgkinson published a formula in 1831 which was used to estimate the failure load for a cast-iron beam resting between simple supports with a centrally applied load (W in Fig 25) (Singer *et al*):

$$W = \frac{26A_b d}{L}$$

where W $\quad$ = centrally applied load at failure (tons)
$\quad A_b \quad$ = area of bottom flange (in²)
$\quad d \quad$ = depth of beam (in)
$\quad L \quad$ = span of beam (in)

No indication was given of the area of top flange required, but other work established that the area of the bottom flange should be six times that of the top flange. With large spans it was found that rapid cooling of the thinner parts set up high internal stresses, thus reducing its load-carrying capacity.

The production of a more ductile form of iron — wrought or malleable iron with a much greater tensile strength than cast iron — was possibly achieved in about 1750 (Singer *et al*) by Abraham Darby II (1711–63). Little is known about the technique involved and the conversion of pig iron to wrought iron by the process of refining, puddling and rolling is generally attributed to Henry Cort (1740–1800). He patented the pro-

121

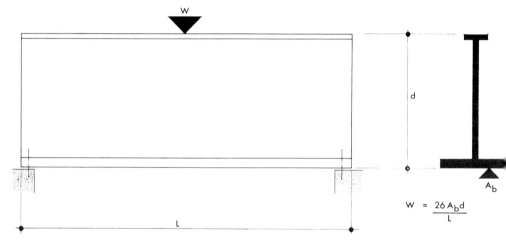

$$W = \frac{26\,A_b d}{L}$$

Fig 25 The inverted T-section was considered to be the optimum form for cast-iron members

cess in 1783–4. The size of section available in wrought iron was much smaller than those used for the cast-iron arch ribs in the Iron Bridge over the River Severn (1779). Typical percentages of carbon and other impurities in cast and wrought iron are listed below:

	Cast iron per cent	Wrought iron per cent
Carbon	2.0–6.0	0–0.25
Silicon	0.2–2.0	0.32
Phosphorus	0.38	0.004
Manganese	0.013	trace
Sulphur	0.014	0.114

The cost of producing wrought iron was much higher than cast iron, as George Stephenson had found previously with the rails for the Stockton & Darlington Railway. The first attempt to substitute wrought iron for cast iron was made by William Fairbairn in 1832. An I-section beam was formed by riveting angles to vertical plates (Fig 26). The heated rivet, with one head previously formed, is passed through the holes in the parts to be connected and the second head hammered on the projecting end. The rivet contracts on cooling to form a tight joint. The two vertical plates (web) connecting the angle flanges were about 6ft 9in (2m) long and staggered so that the joints alternated with each other (G. Drysdale Dempsey). Fairbairn was a friend of the Stephensons and they were no doubt aware of his work. Furthermore George Stephenson appreciated the difference in the properties of wrought and cast iron, as he demonstrated in 1825 with the use of both

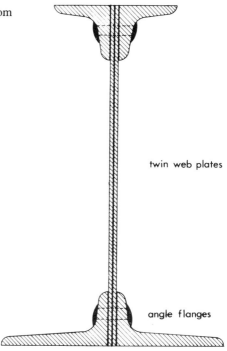

Fig 26 A wrought-iron section built up from flat plates and angles rivéted together

twin web plates

angle flanges

in the Gaunless Viaduct for the Stockton & Darlington Railway (see p38). The form of construction adopted by Robert Stephenson was the trussed cast-iron girder, the general arrangement of which is shown in Fig 27. The rectangular wrought-iron rods were intended to act compositely with the cast iron and assist the cast-iron bottom flange in resisting the maximum tension which occurs at the centre of the beam. The trussed girder was first used in 1831 by Charles Blacker Vignoles (1793–1875) with spans of up to 32ft (9.7m). These were constructed for what became the North Union Railway in 1834 — two in Wigan and one over the Leigh canal at Bamfurlong. Robert Stephenson subsequently designed numerous trussed girders for the London & Birmingham Railway (1836), York & Newcastle Railway (1841) and the York & North Midland Railway (1844–5). They were used by other engineers and

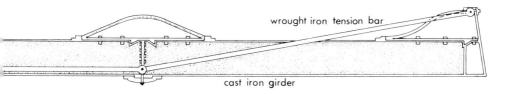

wrought iron tension bar

cast iron girder

Fig 27 The general arrangement of a trussed cast-iron girder

123

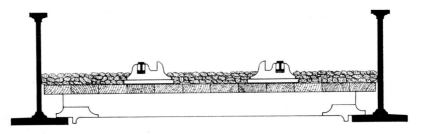

Fig 28 A half cross-section through the Dee Bridge showing the cast-iron girders, transverse beams and decking

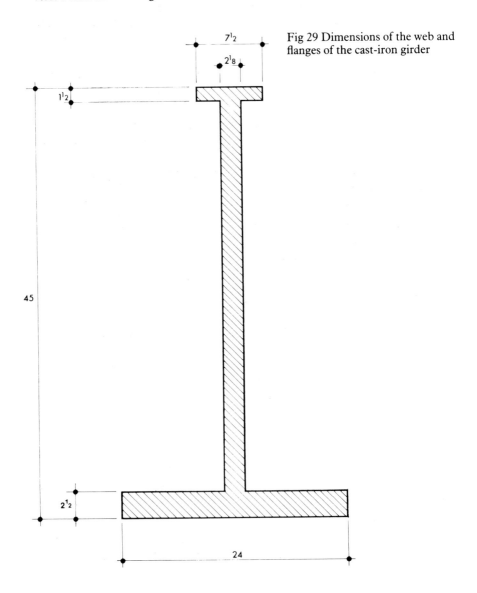

Fig 29 Dimensions of the web and flanges of the cast-iron girder

prior to the design of the Dee Bridge in 1846, the maximum span adopted had been 88½ft (27m).

The Dee Bridge was designed to cross the river at an angle (skew) of 48° with three clear spans of 98ft (30m) between the supporting piers and abutments. Each line of railway was supported by two trussed girders, there being four girders in all; a cross-section of the bridge is shown in Fig 28. The track was supported on ballast placed on 4in (102mm) deep planks which were supported by transverse timbers, seated on the bottom flange of the cast-iron girders. The girders were prevented from moving laterally by wrought-iron rods connecting the bottom flanges.

The complete bridge consisted of twelve girders, each with an overall length of 109ft (33m), giving a 5ft 6in (1.6m) bearing at each end. Fig 29 shows the dimensions of the webs and flanges (moulding omitted) and each girder was cast in three sections. The two joints (Fig 27) were formed by connecting the bottom flanges with wrought-iron clips, bolting the flanges cast on the ends of the webs and providing an additional cast-iron plate 13ft (4m) long and 3ft (0.9m) deep at the centre which was bolted and scarfed (keyed) to the top flanges of the beams. Similar plates of half the length were used at the ends of the three-section girders. There appears to be some confusion over the size of the wrought-iron tension bars. Sibly states they were 6in (152mm) x $^3/_{10}$in (8mm), eight on each side of the girder, and G. Drysdale Dempsey states they were arranged in sets of four, one set on each side of the girder, each bar being 6in (152mm) x 1¼in (32mm). The bars were bolted to the girders at the joint positions, and at the ends they were connected to the girders by wrought-iron keys which enabled them to be tensioned.

The bridge was completed in September 1846 and inspected and passed for traffic on 20 October, enabling the service between Shrewsbury and Chester to commence. It was noticed that the bridge was susceptible to vibration but otherwise its performance was satisfactory.

On the afternoon of 24 May 1847, the placing of a further 5in (127mm) of ballast to protect the timber planking from the risk of fire was completed. The work was personally inspected by Robert Stephenson. The 6.20pm Chester to Shrewsbury train with a locomotive and five carriages negotiated the first two of the three spans but on the third, the driver felt a 'sinking'. He opened the locomotive regulator wide and reached the abutment safely, but a girder directly under the train

Plate 56 An illustration of the collapse of the Dee Bridge (*The Illustrated London News*)

collapsed and the five carriages were precipitated into the river. Five people were killed and a further eighteen of the twenty-five passengers injured.

In 1847, Robert Stephenson was at the height of his professional career; at first sight it is difficult to apportion the blame for this collapse to the engineer who was concurrently responsible for the overall design and construction of two of the finest examples of Victorian bridge-building technique — the Britannia Tubular Bridge and the High Level Bridge at Newcastle. The structural action of trussed girders is complex and in 1847 there was no means of quantifying a design that relied upon the composite action of cast-iron girders and wrought-iron tension bars. Let us consider the factors which could contribute to the collapse of the bridge.

Firstly, the loading: a locomotive and carriages moving across the bridge would induce additional stresses arising from impact and vibration, but it was standard practice at the time to model the train weight by a static load of about 1 ton (10kN) per foot run, uniformly distributed along the length of the deck. To this must be added the self-weight of the deck, amounting to about half the train load, giving a total value in the order of 1½ tons (15kN) per foot run. Thus, an underestimation of the true load effect is quite possible.

A second consideration is that the proportions of the cast-iron girder were based on Hodgkinson's formula (p121) derived from tests on short beams. Applying Hodgkinson's formula with A_b = 66in² (including mouldings), C = 26, d = 45in and L = 1,226in, the distance between the centre of the bearings, then:

$$W = \frac{26 \times 66 \times 45}{1,266}$$

$$= 61 \text{ tons } (610\text{kN})$$

This is equivalent to a total uniformly distributed load of 122 tons (1,220kN) per beam, and thus for a pair of beams supporting the bridge deck, the total uniformly distributed load at failure is 244 tons (2,440kN). The maximum design load for the deck is 1½ x 105½ = 158¼ tons (1,582kN), which results in a safety factor = collapse load/design load = 244/158.25 = 1.54. It was generally accepted that the margin of safety for cast-iron bridges should be in the range of 2–4 and thus the addition of wrought-iron bars was intended to increase the safety factor from 1.54 to an acceptable, but unquantifiable value. Unfortunately, the composite action of the girder and the iron bars was not understood by Stephenson at the time of the design.

A load applied to the composite system will induce tension in the wrought-iron bars and the effects of this at the ends of the beam are demonstrated in Fig 30. The horizontal component (H) of the tension (T) in the bar induces additional compression in the top flange and tension in the bottom flange. Thus, the 7in (178mm) x 1½in (38mm) top flange was subjected to additional compressive forces as a result of tensioning the tie bars. The top flange can be considered as a thin column laid flat with a compressive load at each end. There is no intermediate restraint to prevent the column from moving laterally (buckling) under load, and the danger of this mode of failure is enhanced by initial lack of straight-

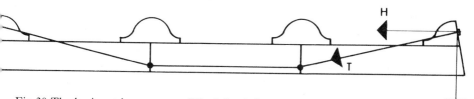

Fig 30 The horizontal component (H) of the tie increases the compression in the top flange

ness of the flanges and the presence of holes. In modern terminology, the failure of the Dee Bridge would be attributed to lateral torsional buckling caused by the inherent instability of the slender, unrestrained, compression flange. To summarise, the factors contributing to the collapse of the bridge are listed below, but the fundamental weakness was the instability of the compression flange.

1 Simple modelling of moving loads by a static uniformly distributed load, no allowance being made for impact.
2 Proportions based on the Hodgkinson's formula for static loads.
3 Lack of appreciation of composite action with the tie bars and the additional compressive stresses induced.
4 Weakness of the intermediate bolted joints.
5 Lack of straightness of the compression flange and the presence of holes cast in it which act as stress raisers.
6 Lack of material homogeniety.
7 Supporting the deck on the bottom flanges which induced un-desirable shear and torsional stresses. Fairbairn appreciated this was a poor detail and suspended the cross beams from both sides of the flange by means of hooks bolted to the cross beams (Fig 31). This avoided casting holes in the tension flange.

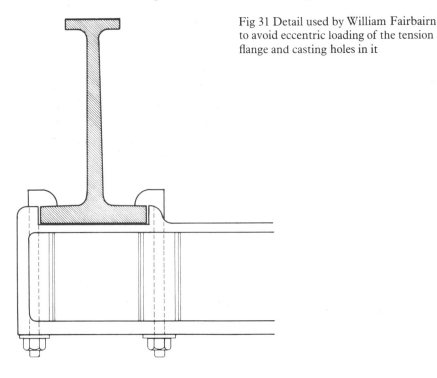

Fig 31 Detail used by William Fairbairn to avoid eccentric loading of the tension flange and casting holes in it

After the accident, Stephenson tested one of the surviving members and it failed at a static load of 38 tons (380kN) (Sibly). Test details were not given, but if taken as a point load, the equivalent uniformly distributed load at failure is 76 tons (760kN). The design load per beam was 0.5 x 1.5 x 105.5 = 79.125 tons (791kN), representing a safety factor in the order of unity. Further quantitative assessment of the structure is given in the Technical Appendix. The bridge was strengthened by bolting additional plates between those at the ends and intermediate joints to give an overall depth of construction along the length of each girder of 6ft 9in (2m).

Robert Stephenson inspected the scene of the collapse on 27 May 1847 and at the inquest gave misleading evidence which was contrived to deceive the jury. He attempted to demonstrate that the beam had failed as the result of a derailment, causing a coach to hit the girder with sufficient force to break a piece out. The jury were not convinced by this explanation and the engineers called in by the Commissioners of Railways to investigate the collapse stated that the cast iron should have been strong enough to carry the total load with a minimum factor of safety of three. This is equivalent to a total uniformly distributed load of about 475 tons (4,750kN) for the two beams supporting the deck.

The jury found that the victims of the collapse were accidentally killed and did not accept that failure was due to lateral load from the derailed train. The bridge and others built in a similar manner were declared unsafe, and this led to the appointment of a royal commission to enquire into the application of iron to railway structures. The commission was appointed on 26 July 1847 and one of the members was Eaton Hodgkinson. Before their report was published in July 1848, a number of eminent witnesses were called in to give evidence, including I. K. Brunel. Brunel's views on cast-iron bridges were well known: 'The number I have is but few, because, as I have before said, I dislike them.'

However, Brunel was concerned that the commission would recommend 'règles de l'art' (conditions to be observed) which would impede progress and referred to the commission as 'The Commission for stopping further improvements in bridge building'. His opinions were expressed forcefully in his letter of 13 March 1838 to the secretary of the commission.

At present cast iron is looked upon, to a certain extent, as a friable, treacherous, and uncertain material, castings of limited size only can be safely depended upon; wrought iron is considered comparatively trustworthy, and by riveting or welding, there is no limit to the size of parts to be used. Yet, who

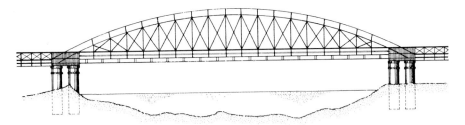

Fig 32 I. K. Brunel's wrought-iron bowstring girder bridge over the River Thames at Windsor

will venture to say, if the direction of improvement is left free, that means may not be found of ensuring sound castings of almost any form and of twenty or thirty tons weight and of perfectly homogeneous mixture of the best metal? Who will say that beams of great size of such a material, either in single pieces or built, may not prove stronger, safer, less exposed to change of texture or to injury from vibration, than wrought iron, which in large masses cannot be so homogeneous as a fused mass may be made and which when welded is liable to sudden fracture at the welds.

The letter continues at length to express doubts about the advantages of the enquiry (I. K. Brunel) and it is of interest to speculate on the form of construction that Brunel might have adopted for the Dee Bridge. One possibility is the structural form he used for the Thames crossing at Windsor in 1849. This was a wrought-iron arch/beam (bowstring) girder bridge (Fig 32) and it is still in service today. The last trussed girder bridges designed by Stephenson were constructed in Italy for the Florence & Leghorn Railway and the 96ft (29m) spans were strengthened in a similar manner to the Dee Bridge. In 1853, Robert Stephenson wrote as follows on the trussed girder (Sibly):

The objection to this girder is common to all girders in which two independent systems are attempted to be blended; and as a general principle all such arrangements should be avoided. It is useless to say more on the subject of this form of girder as, since the adoption of wrought iron for girders they have been entirely superseded. They were designed when no other means existed of obtaining iron girders of great span, and the melancholy accident which occurred at Chester is the only existing instance of their failure.

Samuel Smiles in his eulogy on the lives of George and Robert Stephenson makes no mention of this melancholy accident which occurred on 24 May 1847 and came close to destroying Robert Stephenson's professional career. The design error at Chester should, however, be put in context with the engineering excellence of the Britannia Tubular Bridge crossing the Menai Strait and the High Level Bridge spanning the River Tyne at Newcastle.

6

BRITANNIA AND CONWY TUBULAR BRIDGES

Often at night I lie tossing about seeking sleep in vain. The tubes filled my head. I went to bed with them and got up with them. In the grey of the morning when I looked across the square, it seemed an immense distance across to the houses on the opposite side. It was nearly the same length as the span of my bridge!

(ROBERT STEPHENSON)

Introduction

In the above quotation Robert Stephenson was referring to the wrought-iron tubes of the Britannia and Conwy bridges which were being constructed to carry the Chester & Holyhead Railway over the Menai Strait and the River Conwy. It is difficult to cavil with any aspect of L. T. C. Rolt's definitive and stimulating biography of George and Robert Stephenson, but his final assessment of Robert Stephenson's great tubular bridges is arguably incorrect:

By the time the Victoria Bridge [Montreal, see Chapter 8] was completed it was already obsolete in design, so rapid was the development of technique. In his splendid Royal Albert Bridge over the Tamar at Saltash [Fig 33], which was opened in May 1859, Brunel demonstrated an altogether lighter, more scientific and economical form of wrought-iron construction for bridges of large span than the great rectangular tube.

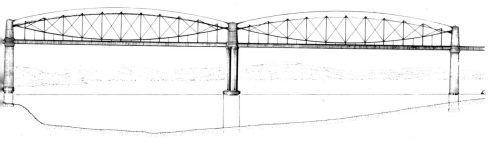

Fig 33 The Royal Albert Bridge, Saltash, designed by I. K. Brunel

131

However, technically, the Britannia bridge remained the most significant nineteenth-century bridge structure, in terms of future developments, for 120 years until the tragic fire, started by two schoolboys, on 23 May 1970. The tubes were so badly damaged that it was necessary to replace them by steel arches. Brunel's ingenious arch/chain system of the Tamar bridge was not repeated, but tubular sections are now common for short, medium and large span structures of both steel and concrete. Their design frequently involves testing of models to ensure a complete understanding of the structural action; the model tests carried out by Fairbairn and Hodgkinson, leading to the optimisation of the structural form, were of great interest to engineers until the period following World War II, when extensive bridge-building programmes involved investigation of the stability of thin walled tubular sections.

The Development of the Tubular Form

All aspects of the construction of the Britannia Tubular Bridge were of an unprecedented scale — the conceptual design leading to the proposal for a tubular form, extensive tests to optimise the distribution of metal in the tubes, detailed structural calculations, fabrication techniques and the floating and lifting of the 1,600 ton (16,000kN) tubes into position and lifting them 105ft (32m) above water level.

Forty years before the completion of the Britannia Bridge in 1850, Thomas Telford was faced with a problem of similar magnitude — to cross the Menai Strait with a road bridge. In 1810, a commission was appointed to report on the state of the roads between Shrewsbury, Chester and Holyhead, and Telford was called upon to submit proposals for bridging the Menai Strait. He initially designed two cast-iron bridges — one at Swilley Rock consisting of three 260ft (79m) span cast-iron arches separated by two 100ft (30m) span stone arches, the stone arches resisting the horizontal thrust of the iron arches. Another at Ynys-y-moch consisted of a single cast-iron arch 500ft (152m) span with

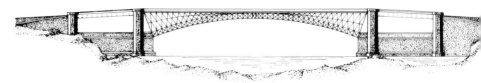

Fig 34 Telford's proposal for a single-span cast-iron arch to span the Menai Strait was rejected by the Admiralty owing to the restricted headroom provided

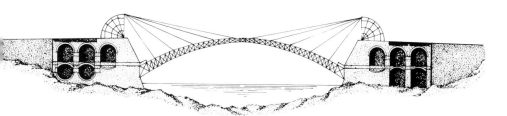

Fig 35 The method proposed for constructing Telford's arch without support from below

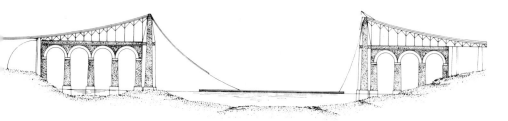

Fig 36 The method used to lift the chains of the Menai suspension bridge

a rise of 100ft (30m) (Fig 34). The method of constructing the arch without support from below is illustrated in Fig 35. These designs were not acceptable to the Admiralty owing to the restricted headroom provided by the arch form and in 1818, Telford proposed a suspension bridge of 579ft (176m) span which maintained a headroom of 100ft (30m) above the whole of the navigable waterway. Extensive tests on wrought-iron chains had convinced Telford of the suitability of this form of construction, and work on the construction was commenced in 1820. Fig 36 illustrates the method of lifting sixteen chains which supported an unstiffened timber deck. The deck was 30ft (100m) wide with two 12ft (3.6m) carriageways and a central walkway. The structure was completed in 1826 — the world's largest clear span (Plate 57). The bridge was susceptible to wind- and traffic-induced oscillations and in 1839 the deck was destroyed by a storm. A stiffer timber deck survived until renewal in 1893 and the chains were replaced in 1940. The bridge would undoubtedly have collapsed if a proposal by George Stephenson in 1839 to lay a single-track railway on one carriageway had been adopted. Horses were to be used to draw the trains across.

Initial proposals for the form of construction of the Britannia Bridge followed a similar pattern to the Menai Bridge. The Admiralty rejected a design consisting of 450ft (137m) span cast-iron arches, as clear headroom of 105ft (32km) above high-water level could not be maintained.

Plate 57 Telford's suspension bridge over the Menai Strait was completed in 1826 and then had the world's largest clear span of 579ft (178m) (*Derrick Beckett*)

Thus Robert Stephenson was forced to consider some form of suspension bridge. He was obviously aware of the unsuitability of a suspension bridge with a light timber deck for carrying locomotive loads. The original conception of a tubular bridge can be attributed to Robert Stephenson (Fairbairn):

... that Mr Stephenson conceived the original idea of a huge tubular bridge, to be constructed of riveted plates and supported by chains, and of such dimensions as to allow of the passage of locomotive engines and railway trains through the interior of it.

In April 1845 there were no drawings or calculations to quantify Stephenson's proposals and he consulted Fairbairn with regard to its practicality. Stephenson's idea was that tubes of circular or an egg-shaped form would stiffen the chains and prevent excessive oscillations of the structure. Fairbairn was opposed to the idea of using chains and it was decided to investigate the matter experimentally, for which

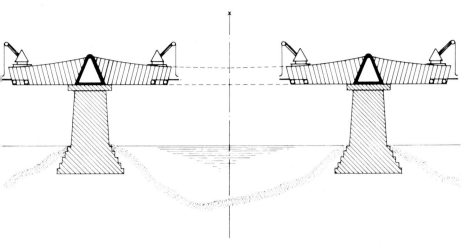

Fig 37 William Fairbairn's proposal for constructing a bridge by building out in cantilever from the piers

Fairbairn was entirely responsible. At this stage of the development of the design, both Stephenson and Fairbairn were of the view that the whole of the tube could be maintained in tension and Fairbairn proposed a catenary form of construction (Fig 37) which could be constructed by building out symmetrically from the piers. This form of construction is now referred to as cantilever construction and has been successfully employed on a number of bridges. However, Fairbairn had second thoughts:

On mature consideration, it appeared next to impossible to maintain the balance of so great a mass upon the pier as a fulcrum, and so to keep both ends in exact line (as regards their horizontal and lateral position), as to cause them to meet in the middle. The plan was therefore abandoned for another of a more tangible kind . . .

Fairbairn reported on the tests on the circular tubes which he found to be 'more or less defective' because of the weakness of the rivet lines connecting the plates and preparations were made for further tests on rectangular or elliptical forms. By August 1845, it became apparent to Fairbairn that the loads could not be transmitted by pure tension in the tubes and that the tubes acted as hollow beams or girders which, if resting between single supports, would develop compression on the top surface and tension on the bottom surface. The tests revealed that the compression surface failed before the tension surface. Thus Fairbairn set about discovering a means of strengthening the tops of the tubes and recommended a rectangular form to replace the circular or elliptical form proposed by Stephenson. The rectangular form permitted

135

stronger connections between the plates, with strengthening corner angles, and greater flexibility with regard to the disposition of the material. Some typical results are listed in Table 3 below and the sections are illustrated in Fig 38.

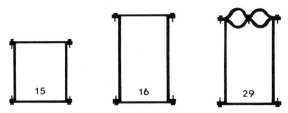

Fig 38 Forms of tubes tested by William Fairbairn. Test 29 gave superior results to 15 and 16 (see Table 3)

Table 3 Typical test results; the form of the tubes is shown in Fig 77.

Test No	Span ft in (m)	Beam depth in (mm)	Width in (mm)	Plate thickness in (mm)		Failure load lb (kN)	Mode of failure
				Top	Btm		
15	17-6	9³/₅	9³/₅	0.075	0.124	3,788	compression
	(5.33)	(244)	(244)	(1.9)	(3.2)	(16.9)	
15a	17-6	9³/₅	9³/₅	0.142	0.075	7,148	tension
	(5.33)	(244)	(244)	(3.6)	(1.9)	(31.9)	
16	17-6	18¹/₄	9¹/₄	0.059	0.149	6,812	compression
	(5.33)	(464)	(233)	(1.9)	(3.8)	(30.4)	
16a	17-6	18¹/₄	9¹/₄	0.149	0.059	12,188	tension
	(5.33)	(464)	(235)	(3.8)	(1.5)	(54.4)	
29	19-0	15²/₅	7.75	0.23	0.18	22,469	sides distorted,
	(5.79)	(391)	(197)	(5.8)	(4.6)	(100.3)	corrugated top

In tests 15, 15a, 16 and 16a it should be noted that the failure load is considerably enhanced by providing a thicker top plate. The mode of failure in compression is that the top plate wrinkles or buckles. Of even greater significance was the result of test 29 in which the top surface was formed of corrugated iron to give a cellular form. It failed by the simultaneous tearing of the side plates from the top and bottom plates at a load of 22,469lb (100.3kN). In this report, Fairbairn expressed the opinion that the tubes for the bridge could be made sufficiently strong to sustain their own weight plus an additional load of 2,000 tons (20,000kN) uniformly distributed along their length:

136

In fact, it should be a huge sheet iron hollow girder, of sufficient strength and stiffness to sustain those weights; and, provided the parts are well proportioned, and the plates properly riveted, you may strip off the chains and leave it as a useful monument of the enterprise and energy of the age in which it was constructed.

During the course of these tests, Fairbairn sought the assistance of Eaton Hodgkinson on the mathematical aspects of the work. Hodgkinson's report gives formulae for estimating the strength of circular, elliptical and rectangular tubes and the results of experiments to determine the correct proportion of metal in the top and bottom of a tube. It ends with the statement:

If it be determined to erect a bridge of tubes, I would beg to recommend that suspension chains be employed as an auxiliary, otherwise great thickness of metal would be required to produce adequate stiffness and strength.

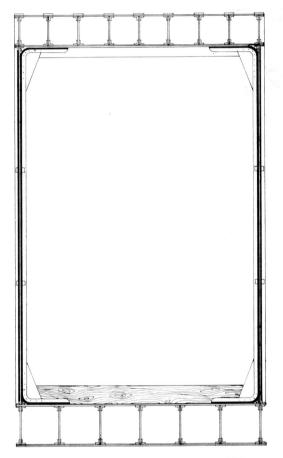

Fig 39 The final form of the tubes with cellular top and bottom flanges — eight cells in the top and six in the bottom

There are conflicting statements in the reports submitted by Stephenson and Fairbairn to the parliamentary committee. Stephenson states that he availed himself of the assistance of Fairbairn and Hodgkinson at the same time, whereas Fairbairn states:

It was I, and not Mr Stephenson, that solicited Mr Hodgkinson's co-operation, and this was not done until I had been actively engaged for several months in my experimental researches, and after I had discovered the principle of strength which was offered in the cellular top, [see Fig 38] and not only proved the impractibility [sic] of Mr Stephenson's original conception, but had given the outline of that form of tube which was ultimately carried into execution . . .

It was not until October 1846 that Robert Stephenson accepted that the tubes could be designed to be self-supporting and this was six months after work had commenced on the foundations of the Britannia Bridge. The final stages of the testing involved the construction of a model of 75ft (23m) span. A cellular structure was adopted for the top (compression) face. With this model, the cellular compression face was strong enough to prevent buckling prior to the failure in tension of the bottom face. The bottom face was gradually increased in area until the strength and compression and tension were approximately equal. The final form of the tubes is shown in Fig 39 and the principal dimensions are given in Table 4 (Fairbairn):

Table 4 Principal dimensions of the Britannia and Conwy bridges.

	BRITANNIA ft in (m)	CONWY ft in (m)
Total length of each tube	1524 (464.8)	424 (129.32)
Total length of tube for both lines of railway	3048 (929.6)	848 (258.64)
Maximum clear span	460 (140.3)	400 (122)
Height of tubes at midspan	30 (9.15)	25 6 (7.77)
Height of tubes at intermediate piers	27 (8.23)	—
Height of tubes at ends	23 (7.01)	22 6 (6.85)
Extreme width of tubes	14 8 (4.47)	14 8 (4.47)
No of rivets in one tube	882,00	240,000
No of rivets in whole bridge	1,764,000	480,000

Extensive calculations are included in Fairbairn's account of the construction of the two bridges and some aspects of this work are included in a Technical Appendix.

Construction of the Bridges

The construction of the bridges proceeded simultaneously and the following approximate dates will help to clarify the sequence of events.

10 April 1846	Foundation stone to Britannia Bridge laid
12 May 1846	Foundation stone to Conwy Bridge laid
March 1847	Work commenced on first Conwy tube
6 March 1848	First Conwy tube floated on pontoons
16 April 1848	First Conwy tube raised into final position
18 April 1848	R. Stephenson passed through Conwy tube with first locomotive
1 May 1848	Conwy Bridge opened for single-line traffic
12 October 1848	Second Conwy tube floated on pontoons
2 January 1849	Second Conwy tube raised into final position
20 June 1849	First Britannia tube floated on pontoons
13 October 1849	First Britannia tube raised to final position
3 December 1849	Second Britannia tube floated on pontoons
7 January 1850	Second Britannia tube raised into final position
5 March 1850	R. Stephenson passed through the single line of tubes on the first train
18 March 1850	Britannia Bridge opened for single-line traffic
19 October 1850	Both lines on the Britannia Bridge opened

Fig 40 shows the general arrangement of the tubes and piers for the Britannia Bridge. The Conwy Bridge consists of two single-span tubes of 400ft (122m) clear span. The tubes are supported on masonry abutments built in an architectural style to blend with that of Conwy Castle (Plate 58). It can be seen that the towers for the Britannia Bridge were built with the intention of supporting the tubes with chains, and slots are provided at the top to accommodate the seatings for the chains. The Britannia tubes were connected at the towers to form a continuous span of over 1,500ft (457m). An ingenious sequence of construction was adopted in an attempt to equalise the stresses along the length of the tubes (see Technical Appendix III).

With a total length of over 1,500ft (457m) it was necessary to provide for thermal expansion. It appears that an estimation of the movement of

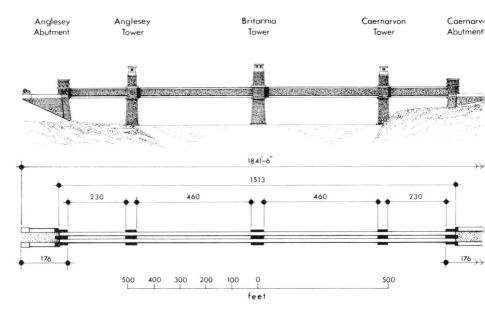

Anglesey Abutment   Anglesey Tower   Britannia Tower   Caernarvon Tower   Caernarvo Abutment

1841'-6"

1513

230   460   460   230

176   176

500   400   300   200   100   0   500

feet

Fig 40 The general arrangement of the tubes and the piers for the Britannia Bridge

Plate 58 The Conwy Bridge tubes are supported on masonry abutments built in an architectural style to blend with that of the castle (*Frances Gibson-Smith*)

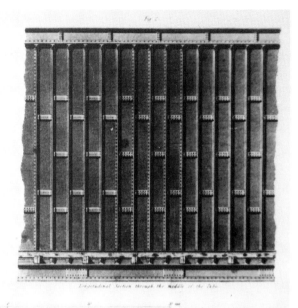

Plate 59 Transverse and longitudinal sections through the middle of a tube of the Britannia Bridge

the tubes was based on the results of experiments on wrought iron by Professor Daniell in 1831 (G. Drysdale Dempsey) who reported that a temperature change of 76°F (24°C) produced a change in length of 1/2000th of the original length. It was considered that the temperature range could reach 100°F (38°C) and thus the increase in length (x) for an original length of 1,524ft (464m) is:

$$x = \frac{100}{76} \times \frac{1524 \times 12}{2000} = 12\text{in (30cm)}$$

This would be the total movement if the tubes were fixed at one abutment and allowed to move freely over the three intermediate towers and second abutment. To reduce this movement to 6in (15cm), the tubes were fixed at the Britannia Tower and roller bearings (Fig 41) were provided at the abutments and outer Anglesey and Caernarvon towers.

A short section of the original Britannia Tubular Bridge has been preserved on the Caernarvon side of the reconstructed bridge (see Gazetteer). Unfortunately, it is surrounded by builders' rubbish (September 1982), but an impression of its scale can be obtained by comparing its height with that of the author standing inside (Plate 60).

141

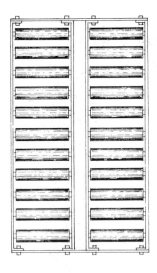

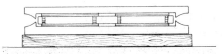

Fig 41 Roller bearings supported the tubes at the abutments and at the Anglesey and Caernarvon towers to allow for thermal movement

The general condition of the 132-year-old wrought-iron components is good, but they are coated with numerous layers of bitumen. The contractors, Messrs Garforth of Manchester and C. J. Mare of Ditchburn & Mare, were faced with the problem of fabricating from wrought-iron flat plates, L- and T-sections, almost ¾ mile (1.2km) of tube for the two bridges. The technique of using wrought iron for structural purposes had its origins in the shipbuilding industry, and the hull of Brunel's steamship the *Great Eastern*, 692ft (211m) long and launched in 1858, has been compared with that of the Britannia tubes (Beckett). The maximum size of flat plate used for the bridges was 12ft (3.6m) x 2ft 4in (0.7m). Further details of the arrangement of the plates and the method of connecting the components are given in Technical Appendix III. Briefly, hundreds of thousands of rivets were required to connect the flats, T- and L-sections — the holes were punched by machine but the heated rivets were closed by hand.

As we have seen, work on the two bridges commenced in the early summer of 1846 and it was proposed by the contractor that the tubes for the Conwy Bridge should be fabricated close to the site, then floated into position on pontoons and raised 18ft (5.4m) by hydraulic presses located in the piers. The floating of the first tube, weighing about 1,300 tons (13,000kN) including castings for lifting, was personally super-

Plate 60 An impression of the scale of the Britannia tube bridge can be obtained by comparing its height with that of the author standing inside (*Frances Gibson-Smith*)

vised by Robert Stephenson with the assistance of Brunel and others. However, the combined talents of Stephenson and Brunel were not a complete insurance against mishap — the pontoons were slightly displaced by the tide and the Conwy end of the tube could not be placed in the correct position. The weather deteriorated and a number of pontoons and five days were lost before the tube was manoeuvred into position. It was possible to raise the tube at the rate of about 2in (51mm) per minute. The floating and raising of the second tube proceeded

Plate 61 G. Hawkin's lithograph of the state of construction of the Britannia Bridge in May 1849 (*Science Museum, London*)

smoothly until it was about 2ft 3in (0.7m) below the bearings (L. T. C. Rolt). A crack appeared in the iron framing of the lifting presses and the tube was supported from below by timber packing. As lifting continued, further packing was added, but the press framing held the load until the tube reached its final position on 2 January 1849.

The floating and raising of the Conwy tubes can be considered as a dress rehearsal for the more formidable task in the Menai Strait which, by January 1849, was the scene of frenzied activity. The main tubes of overall length 472ft (174m) were being fabricated on the Caernarvon shore. This work was undertaken on timber staging at the ends of which masonry piers were erected. On completion of the tubes the timber staging was removed and thus the tubes were unsupported between the piers. This enabled the deflection of the tubes under their own weight, approximately 1,400 tons (14,000kN), to be determined.

The outer tubes, of overall length 274ft (83.5m), were constructed on timber staging erected between the abutments and the Caernarvon and Anglesey towers. G. Hawkin's lithograph (Plate 61) gives dramatic visual impression of the state of construction in May 1849. The central tower was constructed on the Britannia Rock in the middle of the strait. At low tide the rock projects about 10ft (3m) above water level and is covered by up to 10ft (3m) of water at high tide. The Britannia Tower rises to a height of about 230ft (70m) above foundation level. It is of cellular construction and the stones are of durable limestone quarried at Penmaen, close to the site. The internal stones are a less durable red sandstone quarried at Runcorn and the total weight of masonry in the tower is about 20,000 tons (200,000kN).

In June 1849 final arrangements were being made to float the four main tubes. Each tube was supported by eight pontoons of dimensions 98ft (30m) x 25ft (8m) x 11ft (3.3m) deep. Six of the pontoons were of timber construction and had been used for supporting the Conwy tubes. The remaining two were of wrought-iron construction and the first stage of the operation was to arrange the pontoons in groups of four at each end of the tube at low tide. With the rising tide the tube was raised from its bearings. The first attempt to move a tube out into the strait was scheduled for 19 June 1849. Grandstands were erected on the three remaining tubes and an additional stand was provided on Anglesey shore. The thousands of spectators were to be disappointed as one of the capstans used for winding cables failed. The capstan was repaired and by the following evening, the massive tube supported by the eight pontoons was slewed round into the strait and moved at an alarmingly increasing rate under the action of the wind and current.

A further capstan failed, but the supervisor responded quickly to the danger of the situation and a crowd of spectators assisted in holding on to the cable and controlling the movement of the tube. At the Britannia Tower, the tube was guided into a recess provided in the masonry and at the Anglesey Tower, a section of the masonry forming the recess for the tubes was left out which enabled the Anglesey end of the tube to be swung into position. The corbelling above the level at which the tubes were placed is clearly seen in G. Hawkin's lithograph (Plate 61). An even more hazardous operation was the lifting of the 1,600 ton (16,000kN) tube 100ft (30m) to rest on the cast-iron bearers at the top of the recess. This was achieved by using the principle of the hydraulic press which was patented in 1796 by Joseph Bramah (1748–1814). The principle of hydraulic power transmission is illustrated in Fig 42. The volume of water displaced by the smaller ram A moving down through a distance x_1 will equal the volume taken up by the larger ram B moving up through a distance x_2. The work done, that is the product of load times displacement, is the same for both rams and the water exerts an equal pressure in all directions. If the load W_1 is 10 tons (100kN) and the area of ram A is 5in² (3,226mm²), the pressure exerted by the water to move the piston B up is $10/5 = 2$ tons/in² (31N/mm²). If x_1 is 10in (254mm) and the area of ram B is 50in² (32,260mm²), then the load W_2 is $2 \times 50 = 100$ tons (1,000kN) and will move up through a distance of 1in (25.4mm).

The following procedure was adopted for lifting the Britannia tubes. Two presses previously used for raising the Conwy tubes were installed in the Britannia tower and a large single press was installed at the other end of the tube. In order to accommodate the presses above the final

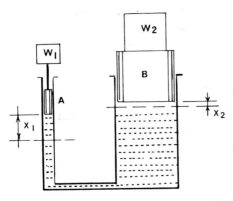

Fig 42 Joseph Bramah patented the principle of the hydraulic press in 1796 which was used as a means of raising the Conwy and Britannia bridge tubes into position

level of the tubes, it was necessary to extend the towers about 100ft (31m) above deck level. The rams were connected to the tubes by chains and the maximum single lift capacity was 6ft (1.85m); water was forced into the presses by steam power. The diameter of the ram for the larger press was 20in (508mm) and it was necessary for it to exert a force equivalent to half the weight of the tube plus additional end strengthening and lifting equipment — about 900 tons (9,000kN). The corresponding water pressure was 2.9 tons/in² (44.3N/mm²) and the thickness of the cylinder walls containing the ram was 11in (279mm).

It will be recalled that the raising of the Conwy tubes was closely followed by timber packing to prevent significant damage to the tubes in the event of failure of the hydraulic mechanism or associated ironwork. At the stage of lifting the first Britannia tube, a young engineer wrote to Robert Stephenson, who was away on other business in London: 'We are now all ready for raising her: we could do it in a day, or in two at the most.' Stephenson's reply was: 'No: you must only raise the tube inch by inch, and you must build up under it as you rise. Every inch must be made good. Nothing must be left to chance or good luck.' (Smiles)

It is fortunate that Stephenson insisted on continuing the practice of using timber packings during the lifts. At about 11.00 am on Friday 17 August, the tube had been raised through three lifts of 6ft (1.8m). Just over one third of the fourth lift was accomplished when the press failed and 50 tons of machinery plunged down on to the top of the tube, killing one man. The potential fall of over 2ft (0.6m) by the tube was reduced to a few inches by the presence of the timber packings. The tube was only slightly damaged but repairs delayed the progress of work by six weeks.

The second tube was placed in line with the first so that when raised, single-line working of the railway could be commenced in March 1850. Seven months later the two lines were operational. When the first tube of the bridge was safely in position, Stephenson remarked to Brunel, 'Now I shall go to bed . . .'; he had not slept for three weeks.

The Fire

The Britannia Bridge remained in service until 23 May 1970 when a fire caused irreparable damage to the wrought-iron tubes.

The following is an extract from a description (1970) by F. W. Hitchinson, OBE, former Caernarvon fire chief:

147

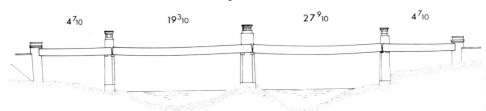

sag in inches

4^7⁄$_{10}$　　　　19^3⁄$_{10}$　　　　　27^9⁄$_{10}$　　　　4^7⁄$_{10}$

Fig 43 The sag of the Britannia tubes after the fire in 1970, from work carried out by Husband & Co, Sheffield

The fire was caused by two schoolboys, who went looking for birds and bats in the upper part of the landbased tower. A hessian tarred strip which covered the recess in the land based tower (where the tubes ends fitted), had worked loose, and the boys further loosened this in order to place their lighted paper to look up into the recess for the birds. This hessian strip caught fire and within seconds the fire had travelled into the upper chamber of the tower. It was not until the fire had burned off the roof of the first landbased tower that it showed itself and a sightseer called the fire brigade. By that time the fire had well travelled through the apertures of the tower onto the underside of the wooden canopy covering the two metal tubes.

An indication of the sag of the tubes after the fire is shown in Fig 43 (Husband & Co, Sheffield) and there was a danger of the tubes slipping off their bearings and falling into the Strait. The chief civil engineer of the London Midland Region of British Rail, consulted Husband & Co, Sheffield (consulting engineers) and the immediate problem was to minimise the risk of the tubes falling. This was achieved by filling the recesses which were originally used for jacking up the tubes (see Plate 61). They were filled with vertically set Bailey Bridge units supplied by the Royal Engineers. Fortunately, it was possible to maintain the towers and, after detailed investigation, it was decided to construct two steel arches under the main spans (Plate 62). These arches were capable of supporting the tubes while they were dismantled. The bottom cells of the tubes (see Fig 39) were still strong enough to act as a rail deck when supported on the new arch below. This facilitated demolition and the top cells and walls of the tube were cut into 15ft (4.5m) long slices weighing 15 tons (150kN) (H. C. & R. W. Husband). A trestle tower supported on a multi-wheeled bogie was pushed under the slice and horizontal cuts were then made which separated the walls from the

(*opposite*) Plate 62 A steel arch of the reconstructed Britannia Bridge springing from the Caernarvon and Britannia towers (*Frances Gibson-Smith*)

Plate 63 The steel arches support road and rail decks but in the reverse order to the High Level Bridge at Newcastle (*Frances Gibson-Smith*)

floor. The trestle thus supported the side walls and top cells and the bogie was then pushed to the end of the bridge where further cutting up took place. The preserved section of tube on the Caernarvonshire side of the strait has been referred to previously. The new steel arches and approach spans support a two-level deck (Plate 63), the railway being carried at the lower level. In order to accommodate the clearance required for road and rail traffic, it was necessary to increase the height of the original openings through the towers. The final form of the rebuilt structure is similar to an arch design proposed by Rennie and Telford at the beginning of the nineteenth century. It is regrettable that more could not have been done to preserve the Britannia tubes, as their conception, fabrication, and erection was unique, but happily the Conwy tubes remain in service.

The couchant lions guarding the approaches to the bridge symbolise the powerful physical presence of the Britannia Bridge, old and new.

(*opposite*) Plate 64 A couchant lion on the Caernarvon approaches, sculptor John Thomas (*Frances Gibson-Smith*)

Plate 65 An early view of the High Level Bridge, Newcastle, before construction work on the swing bridge began in 1868 and before the erection of a jetty between the bridge and the foot of the pier nearest to the camera. The swing bridge was built on the same alignment as all the earlier Newcastle bridges — Roman, thirteenth and eighteenth centuries — the last being Robert Mylne's bridge of 1772–9 which had to be demolished to allow the passage of shipping up river. Mylne's bridge may be seen in the background, and the building to the left of the right-hand pier of the High Level Bridge may be seen in Plate 66 on the extreme right, now painted white (*Locomotive & General Railway Photographs*)

Plate 66 The High Level Bridge, Newcastle. Opened in 1849, the bridge carried the railway on the top deck, while a lower, suspended deck carried a road. Tolls were collected by uniformed North Eastern Railway employees. Until the opening of the King Edward Bridge in 1906, this was the only rail bridge connecting Newcastle and Gateshead. To the right of the High Level Bridge is the famous swing bridge built by William Armstrong in 1876 (*Frances Gibson-Smith*)

7

BRIDGING
THE TYNE AND TWEED

*For God's sake, don't think of taking me down that coal-pit at this time
of night.*

(DUKE OF CUMBERLAND)

Introduction

The Duke of Cumberland was referring in the above quotation to the
steep sides of the Tyne Valley separating Newcastle and Gateshead. To
cross the river, it was necessary to negotiate the narrow winding streets
running down to the bridge at the bottom of the valley.

The Roman presence in Newcastle involved the construction of a
bridge at the low level (Pons Aelu, probably timber), close to fortifications which were erected at the top of the valley on ground now occupied by Newcastle Central Station. By 1400, there was a stone arch
bridge of nine spans with shops and houses built upon it. This bridge
was destroyed by a flood in 1771 (Rennison) and, following the construction of a temporary timber bridge, a similar stone arch bridge was
constructed under the direction of Robert Mylne (1734–1811) and completed in 1780.

Robert Mylne was a master mason and devised an improved method
of lowering the timber centering supporting the stone voussoirs (segments) which was used on the Thames bridge at Blackfriars (1769–
1869). Although Mylne achieved eminence as a civil engineer and architect, his bridge at Newcastle was criticised on the grounds of width
and obstructing navigation. From the time of construction of Mylne's
bridge up to the conflict between Brunel and Stephenson over the route
north of Newcastle (see Chapter 9), there were at least nineteen proposals for spanning the Tyne at the high level between Gateshead and
Newcastle. Brunel's line crossed the Tyne at the site of the present King
Edward Bridge which carries the main line from York to Newcastle.

Following the rejection of Brunel's proposal to link Newcastle and

Edinburgh by an inland route employing the atmospheric system, the Act for the coastal line between Newcastle and Berwick was incorporated on 31 July 1845. This Act included a sanction to construct a bridge over the River Tyne between Gateshead and Newcastle and the opportunity was taken to build a combined rail, road and pedestrian bridge. The River Tyne at Newcastle is 520ft (158m) wide and it was proposed to construct the bridge at a level 120ft (36m) above low water. This required a total length of construction, including the approaches, of about 1,400ft (427m). Thus the scale of the construction is similar to that of the Britannia Tubular Bridge. It will be recalled that by the autumn of 1845 the general principle of the tubular form for long spans had been established (see p136) and thus this option was open to Robert Stephenson for the High Level Bridge at Newcastle.

However, navigational requirements did not require 460ft (140m) spans and Stephenson chose to cross the valley with six main spans of 125ft (38m) (Plate 66) with smaller land arches on each side. In contrast to the rock strata supporting the Britannia piers, Stephenson was faced with a major engineering problem in providing adequate foundations for the High Level Bridge piers as the ground conditions were poor. Each pier supported a total load, including its self-weight, of in excess of 6,000 tons (60,000kN). The means of supporting this load will be described later.

In reducing the main spans to 125ft (38m), Stephenson may have considered 'stretching' the trussed girder principle as used on the River Dee Bridge by a further 25ft (7.6m). Fortunately, this was not done, as a collapse would have been inevitable. The structural principle adopted by Stephenson was to span the 125ft (38m) openings with bowstring girders consisting of cast-iron ribs tied by wrought-iron chains (Fig 44). The upper deck carrying the railway was supported by cast-iron columns rising from the arch ribs. The lower vehicle and pedestrian deck is supported by wrought-iron hangers, again connected to the columns, which in turn transmit the load to the arch ribs. This structural arrangement demonstrated an understanding of the correct use of cast and wrought iron for compressive and tensile load effects respectively, and furthermore the tied arch (bowstring) structural form enabled the piers to be designed to sustain vertical loading as the horizontal loads resulting from the arch thrust were contained by the wrought-iron ties.

(opposite) Plate 67 The six main spans of the High Level Bridge at Newcastle, the upper deck carrying the railway (Frances Gibson-Smith)

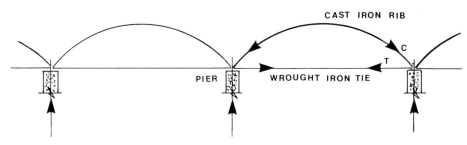

CAST IRON RIB

C

T

PIER   WROUGHT IRON TIE

Fig 44 The principle of the bow-string girder (tied arch). The horizontal component of the thrust (C) in the cast-iron ribs is counteracted by the force (T) in the wrought-iron tie

Construction of the High Level Bridge Foundations

The following description of the construction of the High Level Bridge is based on an appendix to a report of the Commissioners of Railways prepared by Captain R. M. Laffan, Royal Engineers, dated 11 August 1849.

Sir . . . I have the honour to report to you, for the information of the Commissioners, that I this day inspected the High Level Bridge over the Tyne at this place. I shall defer till my return to Town entering into any detailed description of this work and I shall confine myself at present to stating that all the works of the bridge are completed and that I believe it to be perfectly secure and safe. The Company have as yet only laid one line of rails over this structure and I beg to recommend that permission be given to open that one line . . .
I have, etc, R. M. Laffan

As indicated previously, the major enginering problem facing Robert Stephenson was to obtain a firm footing for pier loads in excess of 6,000 tons (60,000kN). The ground conditions below the river bed are shown in Fig 45. The solution was to drive 121 timber piles (for each pier) through loose sand, gravel and clay into the upper layers of the freestone. The foundations to the base of the piers were built up from the tops of the piles.

The first stage of the construction was to build a rectangular structure (cofferdam) for preventing the flow of water into the excavation required to construct the foundations. This was formed by driving two rows of sheet piles 4ft (1.2m) apart to provide a dam of overall dimensions 76ft 6in (23m) x 29ft (9m). The four corners were cut off by 10ft (3m) x 10ft (3m) triangles (see Fig 46). The sand in the gap between the two rows of sheet piles was removed to a depth of 16ft (4.8m) below water level and then filled to a few feet above the high-water level with well-compacted clay. This formed an impervious barrier to the passage

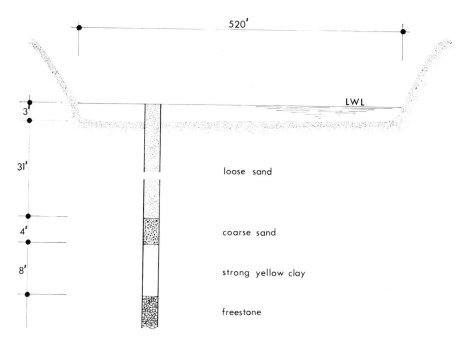

Fig 45 The ground conditions below the river bed. Timber piles were driven by steam hammer into the freestone

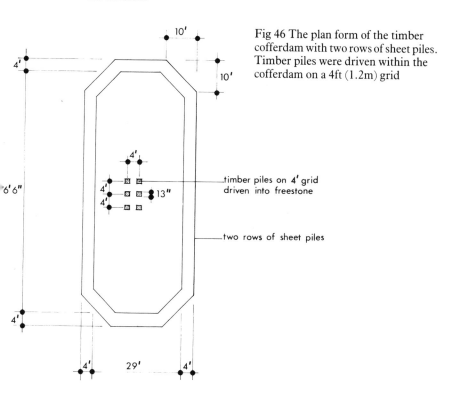

Fig 46 The plan form of the timber cofferdam with two rows of sheet piles. Timber piles were driven within the cofferdam on a 4ft (1.2m) grid

timber piles on 4' grid driven into freestone

two rows of sheet piles

of water, and the sand inside the cofferdam was excavated to a depth of 11ft 6in (3.5m) below low-water level. Timber piles 13in² (838cm²) on a 4ft (1.2m) grid were then driven down into the stone. Pile driving was greatly facilitated by the use of a steam hammer, one of a number of machine tools invented by William Nasmyth (1808–90). Nasmyth was one of an impressive group of machine-tool inventors including Wilkinson, Bramah, Marc Brunel, Maudslay and Roberts. A comparison of the use of the steam hammer and conventional piling will be made in the description of the foundation construction for the Royal Border Bridge at Berwick.

The first pile was driven on 6 October 1846 to a depth of 32ft (9.7m) in 4 minutes (Smiles). On completion of driving the piles, the heads were cut off at 7ft 6in (2.2m) below low-water level. A capping beam of

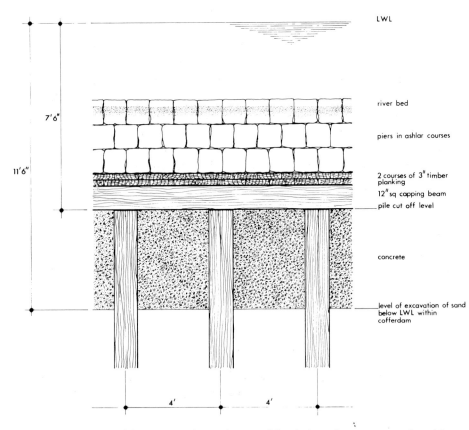

Fig 47 A detail of the construction at the top of the timber piles to support the ashlar piers

12in (30cm) x 12in (30cm) timber was connected to each transverse row of piles. The space from the bottom of the sand excavation was then filled with concrete to the level of the tops of the capping beams (see Fig 47). Two diagonal courses of 3in (76mm) thick timber planking were then laid out at right angles to each other above the capping beams. The inner row of sheet piles forming the cofferdam was maintained and the outer row cut off at river-bed level. Timber boarding was then placed over the clay between the two lines of sheet piles to prevent scour. The foundations to the four river piers resulted in a significant narrowing of the width of water across the Tyne which led to an increase in water depth at low tide from 3ft (0.9m) to 10ft (3m).

The Piers

The piers were built up from the timber planking laid over the capping beams connected to the tops of the piles. A 2ft 3in (0.6m) course of stone (ashlar) bedded in Roman cement was placed over the interior of the cofferdams. This was followed by similar courses of ashlar of the same depth but decreasing in steps of 1ft (0.3m) up to the hollow bases to the twin piers. These bases can be seen in Plate 66 and rise to 2ft 6in (0.7m) above high-water level. The bases to the piers have plan dimensions of 76ft 6in (23m) x 19ft 6in (6m), the voids being filled with rubble masonry. The twin piers, 18ft 3in (5.6m) square were built up from the bases (Plate 67) with an outer skin of ashlar, the void being filled with rubble masonry to a depth of 6ft (1.8m) above high-water level. The hollow piers were then carried up to a solid semi-circular connecting arch below the level of the deck. Each pier is estimated to contain 64,000cu ft (1,792m³) of ashlar, 26,000cu ft (728m³) of rubble masonry and 5,800cu ft (162m³) of Roman cement. The total load, including the superstructure, exceeds 6,000 tons (60,000kN) resulting in a load per pile of about 50 tons (500kN). A pile was test loaded to in excess of 100 tons (1,000kN).

The Deck Structure

The cast-iron arch ribs were placed in pairs each side of the 6ft 4in (1.9m) wide footways (Plate 68) with a central space of 20ft 4in (6.2m) between the inner ribs forming the carriageway. The ribs are of I-section and were cast in five sections, the depth increasing from 3ft 6in (1m) at the crown to 3ft 9in (1.1m) at the junction with the road deck.

159

Plate 68 A view taken along one of the footways showing the I-section cast-iron ribs each side (*Frances Gibson-Smith*)

Plate 69 The hollow cast-iron columns between the arch ribs contain wrought-iron suspension rods which support the lower deck (*Frances Gibson-Smith*)

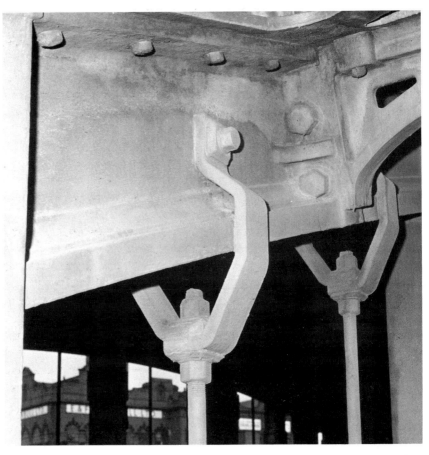

Plate 70 A close-up of the cast-iron ribs and the hangers on the High Level Bridge (*Frances Gibson-Smith*)

The wrought-iron tie chains are of rectangular section 7in (18cm) x 1in (2cm), with eight connecting the inner, more heavily loaded ribs and four connecting the outer ribs. Twelve square hollow shafts 14in (35cm) x 14in (35cm) were cast with, and above, each rib. Square cast-iron columns (Plate 68) of the same dimensions as the shafts rise from the shafts to connect with longitudinal cast-iron girders at the edge of the railway deck. A transverse girder connects each row of four columns extending above the arch ribs, which in turn support the timber structure for the railway deck. This consists of six longitudinal timbers, one under each rail of the triple track, followed by a double layer of 3in (76mm) thick timber planking laid diagonally. The rails were placed on 12in (30cm) x 6in (15cm) longitudinal timber sleepers. The hollow cast-iron columns were extended below the arch ribs (Plate 69) to the level of the ties and contain wrought-iron suspension rods which support the lower deck. The ends of the columns are connected to cast-iron longitudinal girders. The deck is of timber construction with transverse timbers at 3ft 4in (1m) centres supporting a double layer of 3in (76mm) thick timber planking laid diagonally. The footway decking is of similar construction.

There is apparently no complete record of the construction method adopted to erect the deck structure (Rennison), the total weight of iron-work for each 125ft (38m) span tied arch being about 700 tons (7,000kN). Robert Stephenson carried out extensive tests on a number of different compositions of cast iron in order to obtain a mix with the most consistent strength properties. A strength variation of plus or minus 6 per cent was achieved, and casting of the ironwork commenced in the spring of 1847 at the works of Hawkes, Crawshay & Co, Newcastle. Prior to transportation of the ironwork to the site, each arch was fabricated and tested to twice its anticipated loading. It is known that a temporary timber bridge was constructed on the downstream side of High Level Bridge and it was opened for rail traffic in the autumn of 1848. It is possible that the ironwork was transported across the timber bridge and then moved sideways on to timber centering, which in turn

Plate 71 The Newcastle end of the High Level Bridge, showing the road section, looking towards Gateshead (*Frances Gibson-Smith*)

Plate 72 The North Eastern Railway main line terminated with the Royal Border Bridge at Berwick-upon-Tweed, opened in 1850 by Queen Victoria. This view looking upstream was taken in 1913 (*Locomotive & General Railway Photographs*)

was supported on timber trestle piers which were erected between the masonry piers. However, it is known that a transverse travelling crane was erected on a 40ft (12m) gauge track on the upstream side of the bridge, which could also have been used to transport the ironwork.

The bridge, which was opened on 15 August 1849, is in use today but no longer carries the main line from London to Edinburgh; this now crosses the Tyne via the King Edward Bridge a short distance upstream. The views of the more recent bridge structures crossing the River Tyne up or downstream from the High Level Bridge are inspiring, but the engineering excellence and powerful physical presence

of Stephenson's bridge has stood the test of time. A simple quantitative assessment of the principle of the tied arch is given in the Technical Appendix V.

The Royal Border Bridge — Berwick-upon-Tweed

Berwick-upon-Tweed is the most northerly of English towns, a few miles to the north of which the English/Scottish border reaches the sea close to Marshall Meadows Bay. Berwick is situated on the northern shore of the estuary of the River Tweed which is crossed by three bridges.

Work on the first bridge, Berwick Bridge, was commenced in 1611; it carried the Great North Road (A1) until 1926 when an elegant reinforced concrete arch structure was built alongside, the Royal Tweed

Bridge. The Royal Border Bridge, a short distance upstream of the road bridges, was formally opened by Queen Victoria and Prince Albert on 29 August 1850 and formed the last link in the London to Edinburgh railway. The unique architectural features of Berwick are its extensive fortifications and three bridges. The dour sandstone walls of the fortifications, 1½ miles (2.4km) long and 22ft (6.7m) high, have remained intact since they were first completed c1560. The town also contains the earliest barracks to be built in Britain. It is the three bridges spanning the river which provide the most stimulating architecture, in particular the long sweeping curve of Robert Stephenson's arch railway bridge in a setting which rivals that of Brunel's suspension bridge over the Avon Gorge at Bristol.

Of the three great bridges spanning the Tweed, Tyne and Menai Strait, the Royal Border Bridge is technically the least interesting, but its structural form is appropriate to the ground conditions and setting. Stephenson chose to construct the bridge as a series of twenty-eight arches of classical Roman semi-circular form supported on slender piers (Fig 48). Each arch is 61ft 6in (18.7m) in span and the maximum height above the river bed is 129ft (39.3m). The whole of the 2,160ft (663m) long structure is constructed of stone, with the exception of the interior of the arches and piers, which are filled with rubble bonded with lime mortar.

Foundations

The river bed is generally composed of alternate layers of gravel and sand of variable depth. This strata is possibly adequate to sustain the loads from the bridge piers, but it was considered that the flow of the steam would erode or scour the material under the foundation and thus it was decided to build the piers on piles. From experiments it was estimated that the average velocity of the stream was 200ft (61m) per minute (George Barclay Bruce) and thus the discharge in cubic feet per mi-

SOUTH

Fig 48 The twenty-eight 61ft 6in (18.7m) span arches of the Royal Border Bridge over the River Tweed

nute can be determined from the known cross-sectional area of the river at the site of the bridge, approximately 14,300 sq ft (1,315m²).

Discharge = 14,300 x 200 = 2,860,000cu ft (80,080m³) per min

The cross-sectional area of the piers in the water is 2,800 sq ft (257m²) and thus the area of water is reduced to 14,300 − 2,800 = 11,500 sq ft (1,058m²).

A small allowance was made for further loss in effective waterway as it converges between the piers and thus velocity is given by:

$$\frac{\text{Flow}}{\text{effective waterway}} = \frac{2,860,000}{10,733} = 266\text{ft (61m) per min}$$

However, at a velocity above about 215ft (65.5m) per minute it was found that the gravel bed would erode and, dividing the total discharge of 2,860,000 cu ft (80,080m³) per minute by this velocity, the area of channel required to prevent scour is 13,302sq ft (1,223m²). Thus the increase is 13,302 − 10,733 = 2,569sq ft (236m²). The length of the river bed in cross-section is about 800ft (244m) and the increase in depth is 2,569/800 = 3.2ft (97cm). Thus the river bed would erode to a depth of over 3ft (0.9m) before equilibrium is attained and no further scour takes place.

The piers, although piled, were taken down to a level below the probable scour of the stream. As with the High Level Bridge, it was necessary to construct large timber cofferdams in order to facilitate placing of the pier foundations. The efficiency of Nasmyth's steam pile driver at Newcastle led to its adoption at Berwick. Some experiments were made to compare the cost of steam and hand pile driving, which was found to be 2s per linear foot for hand driving and 1s for steam driving. Two species of timber were used for the piles, Memel and American elm. Generally the Memel was found to be too soft and the heads of the piles had to be cut off frequently and rehooped.

NORTH

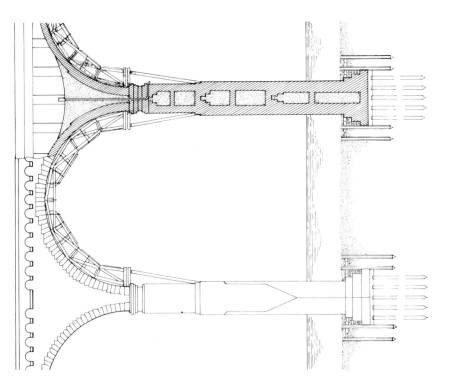

rubble

ashlar

0   10   20   30   40   50
feet

Fig 50 A cross-section through one of the

Fig 49 Details of the piers, arch centering and timber piles

The sequence of operations for construction of the foundations was as follows: the first stage was to construct a temporary timber bridge on hand-driven piles to carry the steam pile driver. The general arrangement of piles (cofferdam and bearing) is shown in Fig 49. The bearing piles were first driven down to the level of the river bed, starting with the centre row and working outwards. The inner cofferdam piles were then driven and the river scoured away to a considerable depth of gravel outside, which reduced the amount of hand dredging required on completion of the outer cofferdam piles. The space between the lines of piles was made watertight by filling it with a mixture of clay and sand kneaded together with water (puddling). The cofferdam was then excavated and the bearing piles driven down to the required depth — up to 30ft (9m) below the river bed.

Considerable difficulty was experienced in keeping the excavation dry and steam and hand pumps were in continuous use. The piles were capped with timber planking above which was placed a layer of concrete.

The Piers

The general dimensions of the piers and their structure in cross-section are shown in Fig 50. A cellular structure was formed of stones cut and squared and bedded in mortar (ashlar) work. A core of ashlar runs to the top of the pier where it meets the springing of the arch. The cells within the piers were filled with rubble bonded with lime mortar. This form of construction provoked extensive discussion when a paper describing the construction of the bridge was presented by George Barclay Bruce at the Institution of Civil Engineers on 25 February 1851.

Robert Stephenson took part in the discussion and acknowledged Barclay Bruce's work on the bridge . . . The whole of the works were constructed under the care of Mr Bruce, and nothing could be more satisfactory than the result:- the bridge stood, without a single flaw, in spite of the rubble being mixed with ashlar . . .

The combination of ashlar and rubble was the principal item of discussion and attracted some criticism. From economic considerations, there was an advantage in using rubble as its cost per unit volume was about one quarter of that of ashlar. The ashlar work involved the use of stones with a volume of about 30cu ft ($0.84m^3$) weighing about 7 tons (70kN), each of which was cut square with the exposed face left rough. They were lifted into position by crane and carefully placed on a

Plate 73 The west side of the Royal Border Bridge from the north end in 1913. Note the extra protection afforded to lampmen by the additional hoops on the signal ladders; it was doubtless quite a business attending to the lamps on the bridge when a strong wind was blowing off the North Sea (*Locomotive & General Railway Photographs*)

mortar bed. The cost of this type of work is obviously high and Stephenson chose to effect a cost reduction by introducing cells of rubble between the vertical and horizontal courses of ashlar (see Fig 50). He argued that the rubble could be considered as independent of the ashlar and merely provided additional means to increase the stability of the piers under the action of lateral loads. This contradicts Mr Bruce's statement that the ashlar was well bonded with the rubble and that the two substances formed a solid mass. In practical terms, the achievement of homogeneity between the rubble and ashlar seems unlikely.

The Arches

The twenty-eight arches were constructed on timber centering, the arrangement of which is shown in Fig 49. The clear span is 61ft 6in (18.7m) and allowing 8ft 6in (2.5m) for the width at the top of the piers, the distance between the centre lines of piers is 70ft (21m). The structural action of an arch is that the compression or thrust in the arch ring (see *Brunel's Britain*) at the springing can be split into a vertical component (V) and horizontal component (H). For a multispan arch with equal spans, the horizontal components of the thrusts due to the weight

170

of the structure balance at internal piers. Thus the pier is subjected to a vertical compressive load (V). However, this equilibrium condition is dependent on all the arches being constructed before the centering is removed. Further, moving loads will induce unbalanced horizontal thrusts. Thus it was necessary to consider the sequence of construction and the influence of train loads as the slender piers have a limited capacity to resist horizontal loads. As Stephenson observed, increased stability is achieved by filling the cells between the ashlar with rubble. The arches at the south end of the bridge were constructed before the piers at the north end were completed and the bridge could not be stayed from end to end to provide stability. Thus it was necessary to exercise extreme care in the sequence of removal of the timber arch centering for re-use on subsequent arches. Three arches were completed prior to the lowering of the rear centering and moving it forward to a new arch. A central abutment was provided between arches 15 and 16 (Fig 48) to enable them to be finished prior to completion of the river arches. Construction of the arches commenced with building up nine stones and filling up the space between with rubble. The effect of this was to raise the timber centres at the crown of the arch and this was relieved by placing bricks at the crown which remained until it was necessary to remove them to complete the arch.

Plate 74 The Royal Border Bridge from a northbound train with a Gresley A3 Pacific at the head (*Locomotive & General Railway Photographs*)

Plate 75 A recent photograph of the piers taken from the Berwick shore. The effects of over 130 years of wind, rain and sea water are beginning to show (*Derrick Beckett*)

With the opening of the Royal Border Bridge in August 1850, there was some relief from the intense pressure of the previous five years — failure at Chester and triumph at the Menai Strait, Conwy, Newcastle and Berwick. The final nine years of Robert Stephenson's life were spent in a lower key, but he was still actively involved in overseas projects in Norway, Egypt and Canada (see Chapter 8).

In contrast, there was no respite for Brunel in the period 1850–9. His projects included the PSS *Great Eastern*, a hospital in the Crimea, numerous timber viaducts and the Royal Albert Bridge at Saltash. The two great engineers survived the last nine years with broken health, and a close personal relationship was maintained. Their deaths were separated by thirty-one days and from 12 October 1859 the prodigious and diverse talents of Robert Stephenson and Isambard Kingdom Brunel as applied to civil, structural and mechanical engineering have arguably not been repeated.

As with the wrought-iron structures at Saltash, the Menai Strait and Newcastle, the Royal Border Bridge has met the British Standard requirement of a useful life, with reasonable maintenance, of in excess of 120 years. A recent photograph of the piers (Plate 75) taken from the Berwick shore demonstrates that all structural materials deteriorate in the course of time and the combination of wind, rain and sea water is beginning to take its toll.

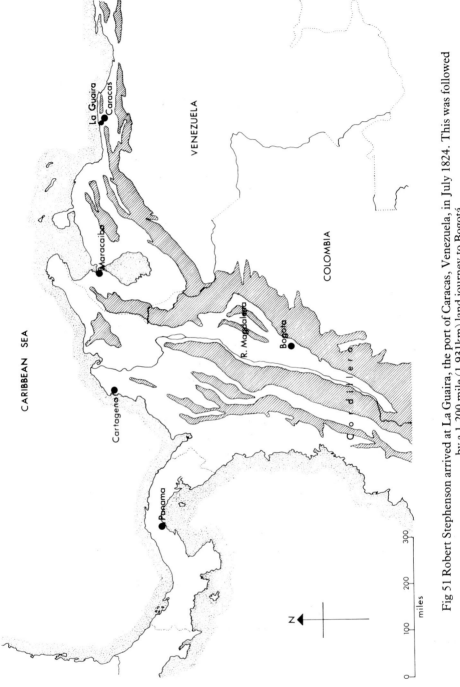

Fig 51 Robert Stephenson arrived at La Guaira, the port of Caracas, Venezuela, in July 1824. This was followed by a 1,200 mile (1,931km) land journey to Bogotá

8

WORK OVERSEAS

. . . when one is travelling about something new generally presents itself and though it is perhaps not superior to some schemes of our own for the same purpose, it seldom fails to open a new channel of ideas which may not infrequently prove advantageous in the end, this I think is one of the chief benefits of leaving for awhile the fireside where the young imagination receives its first impressions . . .

(ROBERT STEPHENSON)

As we have seen, Robert Stephenson left Newcastle in June 1824, leaving the locomotive works of R. Stephenson & Co in some disarray. He had accepted a post of senior expeditionary engineer to the Colombian Mining Association and arrived at La Guayra (La Guaira), the port of Caracas, Venezuela, in July 1824 (see Fig 51). The following extracts are taken from a letter addressed to his parents on 9 August 1824.

We arrived at La Guayra on 23rd July a remarkably fine passage of thirty-five days from Liverpool. The weather was extremely favourable, and with the exception of a few hours calm we had a fair wind the whole way . . . [He describes the climatic conditions and the road between La Guayra and Caracas] . . . the ascents and descents are so steep in many places that I really thought sometimes both the mule and me should have gone headlong down the hill . . . There is a valley which extends between La Guayra and Caracas which is the only situation we can get a good road but even in the valley there are hills as high as Brusselton [Stockton & Darlington Railway].

[RS goes on to reject the idea of tunnelling because of earthquakes] there is no knowing how soon it may come and close it up . . . This circumstance you will agree with me puts tunnelling out of the question — and to make any extensive excavations with high sides would prove equally fatal in the occurrance [sic] of an earthquake . . . I should like to hear from you respecting the way in which you got the Liverpool job finished . . . How are you getting on at Darlington. Remember me to all friends at Darlington . . . your very affectionate son, Robert Stephenson.

In a second letter written on 27 August 1824, but stamped Leeward Islands 15 November 1824, he writes of continuing difficulties in setting out a new road between La Guayra and Caracas and hoped to leave Caracas for Bogotá towards the end of September.

On the 1,200 mile (1,931km) journey by mule to Bogotá, Stephenson was soon to find that he had been misinformed regarding areas reported to be rich in materials. Bogotá, the capital of Colombia, is situated on a plateau of the eastern Cordillera (see Fig 51). Following a meeting with the commercial manager of the Colombian Mining Association, the journey continued, crossing the River Magdalena and on to the slopes of the western Cordillera. The mining district was in the neighbourhood of the old Spanish city of Maniquita. Previous workings were completely overgrown and thus new roads had to be constructed and machinery erected.

The work was obstructed by lack of co-operation from the authorities and a party of drunken Cornish miners who arrived from England — they did not take too kindly to their north-country supervisor. The yield from the mines was not encouraging and Stephenson realised that his three-year contract would be completed before satisfactory productivity could be achieved. The news from England spurred on Robert's return to England. Edward Pease wrote: 'I can assure thee that thy business at Newcastle as well as thy father's engineering, have suffered very much from thy absence, and, unless thou soon return, the former will be given up' (Smiles).

The return journey commenced in August 1827 via the River Magdalena and the port of Cartagena on the Caribbean sea. It was at Cartagena that Robert Stephenson met Richard Trevithick whose fortune in Peru followed the Spanish proverb, 'A silver mine brings misery, a gold mine ruin' (Smiles). Robert Stephenson lent him £50 for the journey to England but both were shipwrecked en route to New York. Following a short tour in the United States and Canada, Robert Stephenson sailed for Liverpool and arrived in late November 1827. He proceeded to Newcastle to rationalise the affairs of the ailing locomotive company.

It is a measure of the international reputation of George and Robert Stephenson that, prior to 1830, export orders were received for four locomotives. The first order, by Seguin Frères and Ed Biot (C. F. de Lyon à St Etienne) was for two 0–4–0 locomotives which were delivered in March and April 1828 at a cost of £550 each. This was followed by the delivery of locomotives to the Delaware & Hudson Canal Co and Baltimore & Ohio Railroad in October 1828 and September 1829 respectively (M. R. Bailey). Each locomotive took about six months to construct. By 1840 locomotives built by R. Stephenson & Co were in service in France, Belgium, Austria, Germany, Italy, Russia and America. This is a record which would be envied by many English manufacturers today.

George Stephenson, initially accompanied by Robert, made a number of visits to Belgium, a country with extensive coal resources and then possessing the densest railway network in the world. King Leopold I (1831–65) was an enthusiastic supporter of railways and consulted George Stephenson on a number of railway projects and the structure of Belgium coalfields. Stephenson was appointed by royal ordinance a Knight of the Order of Leopold — he refused an English knighthood. His last visit to Belgium was in 1845 and shortly after he travelled to Spain to report on a proposal for constructing the Royal North of Spain Railway — a line from Madrid to the Bay of Biscay. En route through France, Samuel Smiles recalls that Stephenson predicted the collapse of a large suspension bridge over the River Dordogne on the road to Bordeaux. A few years later it collapsed under the amplified vibrations of a body of troops marching over it. This is possibly the origin of the rule that troops should break step when marching over a suspension bridge.

In the 1850s it was left to Robert Stephenson to follow his father's example in exporting technical expertise. Following a holiday in Norway in 1845, Robert Stephenson was consulted on the construction of a railway from Christiania (Oslo) to Lake Miosen. Work was commenced in 1850 (L. T. C. Rolt) and Stephenson visited Norway on three occasions (1851, 1852 and 1854) to supervise the works as chief engineer.

Two tubular bridges were built in Egypt for the Alexandria & Cairo Railway. North of Cairo the River Nile forks, one branch reaching the Mediterranean Sea at Damietta. The other branch reaches the sea some 30 miles (48km) east of Alexandria. Both bridges incorporated a central swing beam, one crossing the Karrineen Canal and the other crossing the Damietta branch of the Nile. The Nile bridge consisted of eight spans of 80ft (24m) with a central swing beam of 157ft (48m). The swing beam allowed a clear span of 60ft (18m) each side of the central pier. As the spans were relatively short, the trains passed over the tubes not through them (cf Britannia Bridge). The materials and plant were exported from England.

177

In 1847, Robert Stephenson was a member of a three-man survey team for the Suez Canal project. He made an error of judgement in reporting that 'a canal is impossible — the thing would only be a ditch'.

Victoria Bridge, Montreal

There are a number of parallels to be drawn in the lives of Robert Stephenson and Isambard Kingdom Brunel, the most poignant of which is that they did not live to witness the completion of two of their greatest projects — the Victoria Bridge, Montreal, and the Clifton Suspension Bridge. The Victoria Bridge was opened for public traffic nine weeks after Stephenson's death, but it was not until 1864 that a modified form of Brunel's original design for the Clifton Bridge was completed.

Railway construction in the Montreal district of Canada commenced in the mid-1830s with the 16 mile (25.7km) Champlain and St Lawrence line which facilitated travel to Portland, Boston and New York. A major period of railway development started in 1852 when the Grand Trunk Railway received its charter. Several lines were leased between Montreal and Portland and it was planned to extend the line west to Toronto. The contractors for the Montreal–Toronto section, including the Victoria Bridge across the St Lawrence River, were Peto, Brassey and Betts. Thomas Brassey and Samuel Morton Peto, the most famous English contractors responsible for thousands of miles of construction, joined forces with E. L. Betts for the construction of the earliest of the long-span railway bridges. Included in their terms of contract with the Grand Trunk Railway was the clause, 'when completed [the bridge] to be in perfect repair, and of the best and most substantial character, and to be approved of by the said Robert Stephenson' (K. Jenkins).

In 1852, Alexander Ross, who had assisted Stephenson in the construction of the Conwy Tubular Bridge, visited Canada to inspect the site of the proposed bridge which had previously been surveyed. Robert Stephenson was responsible for the overall design and construction of the bridge with Alexander Ross as resident engineer. James Hodge was agent and engineer for the contractors.

The design constraints imposed on Stephenson were that the large spans should permit the passage of timber rafts, the headroom allowing clearance of the lake boats' masts and the ice-flows which pile up to a height of 40-50ft (12-15m). Following the successful development of the principle of the tubular girder and its application in North Wales, its

178

use at Montreal appeared to be the obvious choice. The overall length including the approaches, was approximately 10,000ft (3,048m). Stephenson proposed twenty-four spans of 242ft (74m) with a central span of 330ft (100m). The wrought-iron tubes were to be supported at a height of 60ft (18m) above river level on massive stone piers. The total cost of the project at about £1.3 million required justification and a possible alternative was, surprisingly, a suspension bridge. Although it was generally agreed that suspension bridges lacked the necessary rigidity to accommodate heavy moving loads, considerable progress in the development of suspension bridge design had taken place by 1850. This was largely the result of the pioneering work of John Augustus Roebling (1806–69) who was one of the most inventive of the nineteenth-century bridge engineers.

Roebling was educated in Europe and his engineering work in America began in 1837 (C. W. Condit). In 1851 he was offered a contract for the construction of the Niagara Falls suspension bridge. The bridge was designed as a double-deck structure, the upper level carrying the Grand Trunk Railway and the lower, vehicles and pedestrians. It was completed in 1855 and was the world's first railway suspension bridge. The span between the masonry towers was 821ft (250m). The metal and timber deck was supported by four 10in (25cm) cables (3,460 wires per cable) and a series of radiating stays. This bridge is referred to by George and Robert Stephenson in the 1877 edition of Smiles' *Lives of the Engineers*: 'The suspension bridge, such as that over the river Niagara, was found inapplicable for several reasons, but chiefly because of its defective rigidity, which greatly limited the speed and weight of trains and consequently the amount of traffic which could pass over it.' However, Robert Stephenson paid Roebling the compliment: 'If your bridge succeeds, mine is a magnificent blunder' (D. B. Steiman and S. R. Watson). In 1896 Roebling's bridge was replaced by a double-deck steel arch as a result of the increased weight of rail traffic. Problems with poor ventilation to disperse engine smoke and increasing rail traffic led to the reconstruction of Stephenson's bridge two years later and thus it came close to being a magnificent blunder.

Robert Stephenson visited Canada in 1853 and the first stone was laid at the bottom of a cofferdam on 22 July 1854. The work-force involved in the construction of the bridge and railway between Montreal and Toronto was massive and the Grand Trunk Railway advertised extensively overseas:

The Grand Trunk Railway company offer to every mason, labourer, blacksmith, and carpenter who will engage to come to Canada to work on the Railway, an advance of £2.10s and £1 for every member of his family, should he have any, on condition of his furnishing security to the local agents for the repayment of such advance at the rate of 1s. per week. The wages offered are — for masons, 7s.6d. to 8s.9d. per day; labourers, 5s; blacksmiths and carpenters, 7s.6d.

Peto, Brassey and Betts received £9,000 per mile (1.6km) (N. E. H. Mika) and claimed to have lost a considerable sum — a common statement today with overseas projects. A large number of workers arrived from England and it was the opinion of the contractor's agent (Hodges) that the English workers were more easily managed and had superior skills to the Canadians but suffered more from the climatic conditions. The climate forced a complete shutdown in the winter and financial restrictions brought work to a halt for almost two years.

The bridge was constructed for a single line of railway, the trains passing through the tubes in a similar manner to the Britannia Bridge. The height of the underside of the tubes above summer water level increased from about 36ft (11m) at the abutments at a gradient of 1 in 130 to 60ft (18m) at the central span. The tubes were supported on massive stone piers. The stones used in the piers were hard grey limestone obtained partly from quarries on the north bank of the St Lawrence, about 16 miles (25.7km) above Montreal, and partly from an island in Lake Champlain to the south of Montreal. The piers were built up from

Fig 52 The upstream face of the piers was designed
to break up the massive winter ice-flows

Plate 76 A photograph of the Victoria Bridge at Montreal, taken on 18 April 1859, showing that the cellular form for the top and bottom flanges was not adopted (*McGill University*)

a solid rock foundation using stones weighing from 5 to 20 tons (50 to 200kN). The rectangular plan form was taken up to about 6ft (1.8m) below the summer water level. On the upstream side, the masonry is taken up at a slope of about 45° to the horizontal, reaching a height of about 20ft (6m) above winter water level. The face of the slope (see Fig 52), was pointed in the form of a triangular cut-water. The construction was strengthened by the use of internal metal clamps. The object of the cut-waters was to break up the massive winter ice-flows moving down the river.

The tubes, constructed on timber staging between the piers (see Plate 76), were 16ft (4.8m) wide and increased in height from 18ft 6in (5.6m) at the abutments to 23ft (7m) at the centre of the bridge. An interesting feature of the construction of the tubes is that the cellular form for the top and bottom flanges as adopted on the Britannia Bridge (see Fig 39) was abandoned. This is clearly seen in Plate 76 and the four walls of the tubes were made up from layers of plates riveted together and stiffened by ribs, gussets and T-sections. Additional stiffening was

181

provided in the central 330ft (100m) span. The tubes were connected in pairs, the centre of each double span being fixed to the pier and the outer ends being left free to slide on rollers placed on the adjacent piers (J. C. Jeafferson). Thus the expansion/contraction length was reduced to that of a single span (see also provision for movement in Britannia Bridge, Chapter 6). The author is not aware of any tests carried out to verify the modified form of the Victoria Bridge tubes, but it is known that the wrought-iron plates, over 9,000 tons (90,000kN), were fabricated in England and shipped to the St Lawrence from Liverpool.

A single line of railway to 5ft 6in gauge was laid on longitudinal timber sleepers in the centre of the tube, with a 4ft (1.2m) footway to one side for access and maintenance purposes. By the summer of 1858, the work-force exceeded 3,000. This and the cost to the Grand Trunk Railway of providing ferries in the summer and sleighs in the winter induced the company to offer the contractor an additional fee of $300,000 if the bridge was completed by the end of 1859 — the scheduled completion date was 1861. The bridge was opened for public traffic on 17 December 1859 following a load test described by the railway commissioners as follows:

The test applied to the tube of the Victoria Bridge consisted of a train of 18 platform cars, loaded with stones as heavily as they could bear, and drawn by two locomotive engines coupled. This train was long enough to reach over two spans at one time, and weighed about one ton to the lineal foot. In passing this train over the bridge a load of 242 tons was laid on each of the side spans, and 330 tons upon the central span.

It was found that two locomotives were not adequate to move the train and a third was required to pull it across the bridge. The deflection of the central span was measured by means of a steel wire and a deflection of 1⅞in (48mm) was recorded under the maximum test load. The recovery was immediate on the removal of the test train.

The Victoria Bridge was officially opened by the Prince of Wales on 25 August 1860 and the ceremony was witnessed by 40,000 spectators. The prince spread the mortar for bedding a 6 ton (60kN) stone at the entrance to the bridge; this being followed by driving home a silver rivet in the central arch. The smell of locomotive smoke does not appeal to all:

Suddenly as one gazes, a hollow rumbling is heard, gradually increasing until with a hellish clang and the reverberation of a million echoes, a train dashes out, bringing with it a taste of the sooty air that lingers in the tubes, the product of fifty years, and abominably like that of an unswept chimney.

('The Holyhead Road log,' c. g. harper, 1902, in *The Menai Bridges*)

Plate 77 All Robert Stephenson's previous work was eclipsed by the scale of the Victoria Bridge over the St Lawrence River at Montreal, his last great engineering work. The ironwork for the twenty-five sections was produced at the Canada Ironworks in Birkenhead

Harper was referring to the Britannia Bridge, but the Victoria Bridge tubes were five times as long as those for the Britannia and smoke was a major nuisance. The slot formed in the top of the tube was not effective and it is recorded that the summer temperature inside the tubes reached 125°F (52°C).

The tubes were replaced in 1898 by a triangulated girder bridge. The inclined cut-waters were built up and the new girders constructed round the tubes which were subsequently removed. In the 1940s the stone piers were strengthened by pressure grouting.

9

THE STEPHENSONS
AND THE BRUNELS

'What do you want to be? . . . *'An engineer.'*

Education

Marc Isambard Brunel's desire, at the age of eleven, to become an engineer did not impress his father, who declared: 'You will only benefit the world and starve yourself' (Clements). There is more than an element of truth in this statement, and although Marc from the age of eight had displayed a talent for mathematics, drawings and mechanics, his father felt that his son should enter the Church. He was sent to the Seminary of Sainte Nicaise at Rouen, but ecclesiastical matters were of little interest to him and he responded to more practical skills — carpentry, ship construction and lifting tackle. Fortunately, the superior recognised that Marc's practical talents should be encouraged, and arrangements were made for him to lodge with an elder cousin and be tutored for entry into the Navy as an officer cadet. Marc was tutored by Vincent Dulague, Professor of Hydrography at the Royal College, Rouen, and Gaspard Monge, who was a gifted mathematician and teacher. He responded well to the best mathematical training available in Europe at that time, and after his third trigonometry lesson verified the height of Rouen Cathedral with a home-made theodolite. At the age of seventeen, his formal education was completed and in 1786 he embarked on a six-year naval career.

In contrast, George Stephenson at the age of seventeen was unable to read or write, but he appreciated that in order to learn more of the work of others it was necessary to become literate. He attended a night school three times a week run by a teacher, Robin Cowens, in Walbottle. The quality of teaching was poor and at the age of nineteen Stephenson achieved little more than the ability to write his own name. Subsequently he attended a night school run by Andrew Robertson in the village of Newburn, nearer to his place of work. According to Smiles,

Plate 78 The Literary and Philosophical Society of Newcastle-upon-Tyne played an important part in the education of the Stephensons (*Frances Gibson-Smith*)

'he took to figures so wonderful' and soon became well advanced in arithmetic. His progress with the 'three R's' was probably very limited, but Stephenson was able to sign the register at his wedding to Frances Henderson in November 1802. In a similar manner to Marc Brunel, George Stephenson developed his mechanical inventiveness through a wide range of practical activities, including modelling engines and repairing clocks. Considerable time was expended on solving the mystery of perpetual motion (Smiles), but he subsequently realised that the ability to read at an early age would have avoided wasting so much effort. Determined that his son Robert should not suffer the disadvantages of illiteracy, George Stephenson paid great attention to his son's education, which started at the village school in Long Benton.

At the age of twelve Robert was transferred to a private school run by Dr Bruce at Percy Street in Newcastle, some 5 miles (8km) from his home. His father bought him a donkey for the journey. Robert's education did not end on returning from school; there were questions on his lessons and demands on him to assist his father with a continuous stream of inventions. Robert was instrumental in furthering his father's education, in particular through Newcastle's Literary and Philosophical Society (Lit & Phil) which was founded in 1793 (Plate 78). Books on science and mechanics were borrowed by Robert and long extracts read to his father. Robert was also taught to read plans and drawings and his father observed, 'a good drawing or plan should always explain itself' (Smiles). At the time Robert was at Dr Bruce's school, his father suggested to him that during the holidays he should construct a sun-dial to be placed over the cottage door at West Moor. After much study and calculation it was drawn out on paper and then carved in stone. In Smiles' *Lives of the Engineers*, Vol 3, a sketch shows the date as 11 August MDCCCXVI but a recent photograph of Dial Cottage shows the date as simply MDCCCXVI (Plate 79).

In 1820 (according to Smiles, see Chapter 2) Robert Stephenson was sent to Edinburgh University and studied chemistry, natural history, natural philosophy and geology. The six-month study period cost George Stephenson the princely sum of £80, but there is little doubt that Robert's scientific background made a significant contribution to the success of George and Robert Stephenson's work on the development of railways in the following two decades.

Returning to the Brunels, Isambard Kingdom inherited his father's talent for drawing and mathematics, and his formal education started at Dr Morell's boarding school at Hove. Spare time was spent in survey-

Plate 79 The sundial over the door of the cottage at Killingworth designed by the Stephensons (*Frances Gibson-Smith*)

ing the town and sketching its buildings and he predicted the fall of part of a new building under construction opposite his school at Hove (L. T. C. Rolt). At the age of fourteen, Isambard Kingdom was sent to the College of Caen in Normandy. This was followed by a period at the Collège Henri-Quatre in Paris, famous for its teaching of mathematics. Finally, a period of apprenticeship was spent under the talented instrument maker, Louis Breguet. At the age of sixteen, Brunel returned to England to work in his father's office in London.

It is of interest to note that the formal education of Marc Brunel, Isambard Kingdom Brunel and Robert Stephenson did not extend beyond the age of seventeen and that of George Stephenson's, if it can be called formal education, did not start until the age of eighteen. The common theme in their education is that of practical application at an early age. Robert Stephenson attributed much of his success as an engineer to Dr Bruce's tuition: 'for it was from him that I derived my taste for mathematical pursuits and the facility I possess of applying this kind of knowledge to practical purposes and modifying it according to circumstances' (Smiles).

Robert Stephenson did not believe in pumping education into the 'working classes' but considered that the artisan required a special education for his own particular speciality and the more he left everything else alone the better (L. T. C. Rolt). Brunel made an even more provocative statement in declaring that he preferred his enginemen to remain illiterate as a formal education only caused their minds to wander from the responsible job in hand. His views on practical mechanics were most forcefully expressed:

I must strongly caution you against studying practical mechanics among French authors — take them for abstract science and study their statics, dynamics geometry etc etc to your hearts content but never even read any of their works on mechanics any more than you would search their modern authors for religious principles. A few hours spent in a blacksmiths and wheelwright's shop will teach you more practical mechanics — read English books for practice — there is little enough to be learnt in them but you will not have to unlearn that little . . . (I.K.B. DEC. 1848)

Samuel Smiles describes the Stephensons as inventive, practical and sagacious and the Brunels as ingenious, imaginative and daring. Of the four great engineers, it can be argued that Marc Brunel was the most inventive. Between 1799 and 1825, he filed numerous patent specifications, including a machine for writing and drawing, ships' blocks, wood-working machinery, shoes and boots, printing plates, copying presses, marine steam engines and gas engines. The Stephensons also filed patents in connection with locomotive design, but in contrast Isambard Kingdom Brunel spoke at length against patents as he considered they retarded the progress of technology.

Professional Relationship

In 1833 Isambard Kingdom Brunel was appointed engineer to the proposed Great Western Railway (GWR) between Paddington and Bristol and by this time the Stephensonian lines — Stockton & Darlington (1825), Liverpool & Manchester (1830), Leicester & Swannington (1832) — had been completed and the London & Birmingham railway sanctioned (1833). The gauge of 4ft 8½in adopted by the Stephensons was somewhat arbitrarily based on the width required for a horse to walk within the rails of wagonways, and as late as the construction of the London & Birmingham Railway stone blocks were being specified to carry the rails.

It required a man of Brunel's confidence and arrogance to challenge the Stephensons' basic railway-engineering principles, and this he proceeded to do with the GWR by adopting a 7ft gauge continuously supported on timber. Again the distance of 7ft between the rails can be considered as arbitrary; Brunel produced impressive arguments to justify it, but its potential for increasing the size of locomotive boilers was never fully exploited. By the end of 1835, the 7ft 'broad gauge' represented about 12 per cent of the total mileage sanctioned. The GWR bill was brought before the House of Commons in 1834 and the committee investigations lasted fifty-seven days. It could be anticipated that this was to be the start of bitter opposition by the Stephensons, but this was not the case. The inconvenience of break of gauge was completely overlooked and at one stage a joint London terminus for the GWR and London & Birmingham Railway was proposed. However, the problem of the meeting of the two gauges was conveniently resolved by the decision of the Great Western board to obtain a separate entry into London.

Brunel's route from London to Bristol via Maidenhead, Reading, Swindon, Chippenham and Bath met with fierce opposition, particularly from landowners, and George Stephenson was called in to give evidence. In it, George Stephenson stated that he did not know any existing line so good as that proposed by Mr Brunel: 'I can imagine a better line, but I do not know of one so good' (Smiles). During Stephenson's cross-examination he lost patience with counsel's questions:

MR STEPHENSON: I wish you had a little engineering knowledge — you would not talk to me so.
COUNSEL: I feel the disadvantage.
MR STEPHENSON: I am sure you must.

The GWR Bill received royal assent in August 1835 and the first section, between Paddington and Maidenhead, was opened in 1838. The locomotive specifications laid down by Brunel were, to say the least, inadequate and the general performance of the first engines delivered to the GWR was poor. In 1837, Daniel Gooch (1816–89), who had previously served an apprenticeship at R. Stephenson & Co's works at Newcastle, obtained the post of locomotive superintendent to the GWR. Gooch's experience of locomotive construction proved invaluable to Brunel but the first reliable locomotive delivered to the GWR was the *North Star*, built by Brunel's great rivals at their Forth Street works. Gooch wrote: 'The *North Star* was the most powerful one, and in other respects the best. She was my chief reliance.'

The *North Star* was one of two engines built by R. Stephenson & Co for the New Orleans Railway of America to a 5ft 6in gauge but not delivered on account of financial problems. The engine was modified to suit the 7ft gauge prior to delivery by barge to Maidenhead in November 1837. Brunel praised the *North Star* as follows:

Lastly, let me call your attention to the appearance — we have a splendid engine of Stephensons', it would be a beautiful ornament in the most elegant drawing room and we have another of Quaker-like simplicity carried even to shabbiness but very possibly as good an engine, but the difference in care bestowed by the engine man, the favour in which it is held by others, even oneself, not to mention the public, is striking. A plain young lady however amiable is apt to be neglected. Now your engine is capable of being made very handsome, and it ought to be.

Twelve locomotives of the Star class were brought into use by the GWR and it is of interest to speculate how Brunel's broad gauge railway, which he considered to be the 'best that imagination could devise', would have fared without the contribution of R. Stephenson & Co and Daniel Gooch. In spite of the eventual successful performance of the Stephenson locomotives on the GWR, the change in gauge did not go unchallenged and, amongst others, Robert Stephenson was asked to comment on Brunel's line. He declined to do so on the grounds that he did not want to become involved in a professional controversy. In July 1844, a royal commission was set up to examine the gauge question and their report was presented to Parliament in 1846. Brunel and Gooch as witnesses presented a powerful case for the broad gauge, but in August 1846 an Act was passed for regulating the gauge of railways which made it 'unlawful to construct any new passenger railway on any other gauge than 4ft 8½in in England, and 5ft 3in in Ireland. Exceptions, however, were made in favour of certain lines in the west of England and South Wales' (I. Brunel). Thus the Stephenson gauge of 4ft 8½in became the standard gauge.

In addition to the broad gauge, Brunel made an even more dramatic challenge to the Stephenson railway system in his involvement with the atmospheric system to replace the steam locomotive, and proposals were made to adopt it on the Chester & Holyhead Railway, the Newcastle & Edinburgh Railway and the South Devon Railway. Brunel was engineer for the South Devon Railway between Exeter and Plymouth, and the Act for its construction received royal assent in July 1844. Financial restrictions forced Brunel to depart from the shallow gradients adopted on the bulk of the line between Paddington and Exeter and gradients as severe as 1 in 40 were adopted. The force required to pull a given load on a gradient of 1 in 40 is seven times that required on the level, and as the locomotive formed a substantial part of the total train load, Brunel recommended to the directors of the SDR that the fixed-engine atmospheric system should be adopted. Robert Stephenson was aware of the limited ability of locomotives to haul loads up inclines and adopted fixed engines to haul trains by rope up the steep gradient from Euston to Camden Town on the London & Birmingham Railway.

The atmospheric system is described in *Brunel's Britain* (Beckett), the principle being that the force created by a partial vacuum pulls a piston along a pipe laid between the rails which has a continuous slot at the top. The slot is sealed by a reinforced leather flap valve and the piston is connected by a plate to the carriage above. The vacuum is created by stationary engines working air pumps placed at intervals along the line. The system was patented in 1839 by Mr Samuel Clegg and Messrs Jacob and Joseph Sumuda, and used on the Dalkey extension of the Dublin & Kingstown Railway.

George Stephenson dismissed the atmospheric system in seven words: 'It won't do' and 'A rope of sand'. Robert adopted a more scientific approach and prepared a report on the atmospheric railway system based on the Dalkey railway and the incline between Camden Town and Euston. This report, which foresaw the technical difficulty of keeping the pipe airtight, persuaded the Chester & Holyhead Railway to abandon the atmospheric system. The Stephensons were faced with a sterner task in avoiding the use of the atmospheric system north of Newcastle. Two routes were proposed for the line which, in 1850, was to connect London and Edinburgh via Newcastle.

George Stephenson carried out a preliminary survey for both routes — a shorter inland route following the valley of the North Tyne through the Cheviots, and a longer coastal route with easier gradients passing through Morpeth, Alnmouth and Berwick. Stephenson's preference was for the coastal route, but no further progress was made until 1843. At this stage the coastal route was vigorously opposed by Lord Howick as the line passed close to Howick Hall, north of Alnmouth. Lord Howick engaged the services of Isambard Kingdom Brunel to support the inland route and to employ the atmospheric system. Samuel Smiles describes the meeting of Brunel and Stephenson at Newcastle:

he good naturedly shook him [Brunel] by the collar, and asked 'What business he had north of the Tyne'. George gave him to understand that they were to have a fair stand-up fight for the ground, and, shaking hands before the battle like Englishmen, they parted in good humour.

The two schemes went before parliament in 1845 with evidence given by Brunel and Robert Stephenson. The coastal scheme was approved by parliament and thus for the second time in a decade Brunel's plans to depart from the Stephenson's principles of railway construction were defeated, and with every justification. Brunel managed to open 15 miles (24km) of atmospheric railway between Exeter and Teignmouth in September 1847 but was soon to admit defeat. The system was abandoned in September 1848 and the line was worked by locomotives.

Brunel's two defeats did not influence his warm personal relationship with Robert Stephenson, and it was in March 1848 that he assisted Stephenson with the floating on pontoons of the tubes for the Conwy Tubular Bridge (see Chapter 6). Nine years later Stephenson advised Brunel on the sideways launch of the *Great Eastern* into the River Thames, which was acknowledged in a memorandum of a verbal report made to the directors and a meeting of the principal proprietors in December 1857: 'That after full consideration of all the circumstances, and assisted by the best advice I could call to my aid, namely, that of my friend Robert Stephenson, I consider . . .'. The two engineers dined together for the last time on Christmas Day 1858 at the Hotel d'Orient in Cairo. Both were in poor health and neither survived the following year. In November 1859, at the first meeting of the Institution of Civil

Engineers after the deaths of Stephenson and Brunel, the president, Joseph Locke, spoke at length on their achievements (I. Brunel) and concluded:

We, at least, who are benefited by their successes, who feel that our Institution has reason to be proud of its association with such names as Brunel and Stephenson, have a duty to perform, and that duty is, to honour their memory and emulate their example.

10

THE STEPHENSONS' LEGACY

To examine the finances of the railway and associated operations, in the light of all relevant considerations, and to report on options for alternative policies, and their related objectives, designed to secure improved financial results in an efficiently run railway in Great Britain over the next 20 years.
(Terms of reference of the Serpell Comittee on the review of railway finances)

One hundred and sixty years prior to the publication of the Serpell Report on railway finances, T. Gray in *Observations on a General Iron Way* produced a diagram of proposed railways in Great Britain (Plate 80). If Falmouth, Plymouth and Holyhead (intended to form rail/sea links) are omitted from Gray's plan, there is a remarkable similarity between the 1822 plan and the highly controversial 'Option A Network' in the Serpell Report (see Fig 53). Option A contains only 1,630 route miles (2,623km) showing a total passenger/freight profit of £34 million. Ten years after the publication of Gray's plan, the total route mileage was only 170 (273km) and the subsequent escalation and decline of the railway network is shown in Table 5.

Table 5 shows that in the first decade of the Stephenson era, the Option A mileage was exceeded with contributions from the Stephensons, I. K. Brunel, J. Locke and J. U. Rastrick and others. By the end of the era (1860) the Stephensons were associated with the construction of trunk routes connecting London and Birmingham; Birmingham, Derby, Sheffield, Leeds and York; Newcastle and Berwick; Leeds, Manchester and Liverpool; and Chester and Holyhead. The complete railway network at this time had required the construction of over 25,000 bridges. George and Robert Stephenson pioneered the growth of a new transportation system which rapidly annihilated competition from the stage coach and canals. Today, the situation is entirely different; British Rail has faced, for two decades, fierce — and many contend, unequal — competition from road interests coupled with mounting operational and maintenance costs. Their civil engineers are now responsible for 44,000 bridges, 700 tunnels and about 3,000 stations and depots with an expenditure of £573 million in 1981 (1982 prices). Over 50 per cent of this expenditure was allocated to track renewals, maintenance and ballasting. In contrast to the first inter-city line (1830) with rails weighing about 35lb/yd (17.36kg/m), the current track utilises continuous welded rails (113lb/yd [56.05kg/m]) on concrete sleepers. This type of track is cheaper to install and maintain than jointed track on timber sleepers. The life of a softwood sleeper is about 25 years.

Table 5

Year		Approximate route mileage	(km)
1832 ⎤	Stephenson	170	(273km)
1841 ⎥	era	1,800	(2,897km)
1851 ⎦		6,800	(10,943km)
1860		7,500	(12,070km)
1900		15,000	(24,139km)
1914		20,000	(32,186km)
1947	Nationalisation	—	—
1962		17,500	(28,162km)
1963	Beeching Report	—	—
1969		12,100	(19,472km)
1973		11,300	(18,185km)
1982		10,800	(17,380km)
1983	Serpell Report	—	—
	Serpell Option A	1,630	(2,623km)

The Serpell Committee comprised a civil servant, an industrialist, an accountant and a consulting engineer with extensive experience of highway works. Unfortunately, the report was solely concerned with railway finances and not transport policy. It proposed a number of options (not closure proposals) for improving British Rail's financial results and was critical of aspects of their management, engineering and maintenance and repair procedures. Even the most ardent British Rail enthusiast would concede that there is room for extensive improvement, but unfortunately the Option A network was, not unnaturally, given massive publicity by the media. The impression was given to the general public that the options were proposals for closure. The report was clearly damaging to British Rail's campaign for high investment and it could be argued that the Option A network is socially and politically unacceptable. A disquieting feature of the Serpell Report is that international comparisons with other railways are completely ignored. In a number of European countries there is heavy investment in rail-

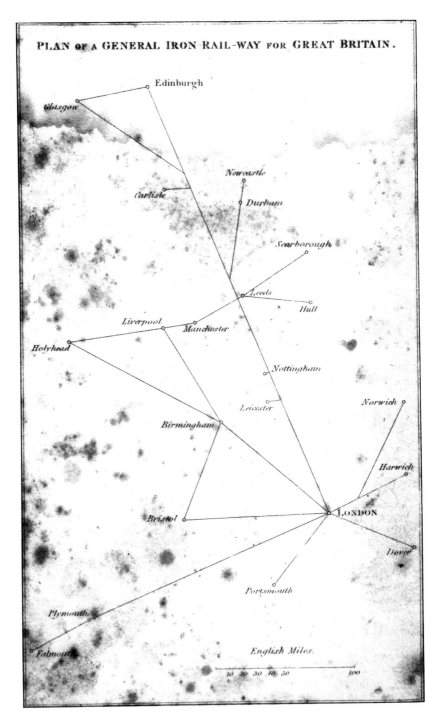

Plate 80 T. Gray's plan of a general iron railway for Great Britain 1822

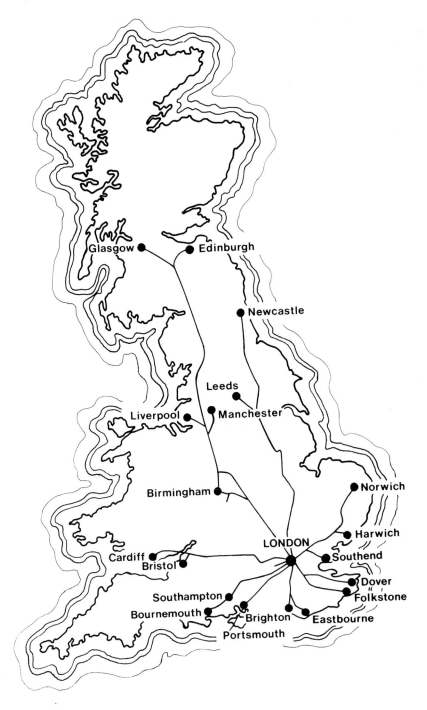

Fig 53 The Option A Network in the Serpell Report published in February 1983. It contains 1,630 route miles (2,623km)

ways, indicating confidence that they will form an essential part of national transportation systems in the twenty-first century.

Successive British governments have failed to tackle the problem of developing a more integrated national transportation system involving motor cars, buses, trains, aeroplanes and more recent developments such as monorails and magnetic levitation. In recent years the railway network has been treated as a poor relation of the road network in which there is a huge vested interest. The wife of one of the members of the Serpell Committee stated: 'George Stephenson has a lot to answer for. I could willingly give him a Rocket' — but so has Henry Ford a lot to answer for. The motor car has ravaged both urban and rural environments and is arguably one of the most selfish of man-made artefacts. George and Robert Stephenson developed a transportation system that can be environmentally kind and energy efficient, and which, at its best, is still the most civilised method of travel, allowing the passenger to commute rapidly between city centres with the options of sleeping, eating, drinking, working or just relaxing. No other transportation system can equal this, but maintaining and improving standards can only be achieved by high investment, and the decline of standards on other than the principal inter-city routes is cause for concern. In the unlikely event of implementation of the Option A network, Robert Stephenson's magnificent bridges in North Wales and the Royal Border Bridge at Berwick-on-Tweed would no longer form part of British Rail's network and would be left to decay. To take the cynical view, this would relieve British Rail of substantial repair and maintenance costs.

It is of interest to reflect on what might have been George Stephenson's reaction to the Serpell Report; it might well have been similar to his reaction to Brunel's proposed atmospheric line north of Newcastle — 'It won't do'.

Perhaps the most important single legacy of the Stephensons' is the 'standard gauge' of 4ft 8½in which was first established on the Willington Colliery wagonway system. It was here that George Stephenson built his first locomotive and went on with his son to establish a viable transportation system using the standard gauge and arguably 'gave railways to the world'. The standard gauge is used in Great Britain, Canada, USA, most of Europe, North Africa, the near eastern countries, China and parts of Japan, Australia and South America. The Stephensons' technical expertise led directly and indirectly to Britain earning millions of pounds in exports — a key element in our Victorian economy and still a major industry.

GAZETTEER

This gazetteer is not intended to include all places of interest associated with the lives of George and Robert Stephenson, which would occupy a complete volume, but rather to select a number of principal locations with the greater emphasis on the civil engineering works of Robert Stephenson. As with *Brunel's Britain*, London has been chosen as the starting point for all journeys. Data on road distances and train times is summarised in Table 6 and the author has visited most of the sites by both road and rail. Time spent in planning a route is well worth the effort and it can be seen from the table that one-day trips are not always practical. In planning a route by car the Ordnance Survey Routeplanner of Great Britain 1982, scale 1:625000 (about 1in to 10 miles or 4cm to 25km) is most helpful as it is especially designed for the advance planning of long-distance journeys and business and pleasure motoring. Details of all Ordnance Survey publications are available free on request from Ordnance Survey (Information and Enquiries), Romsey Road, Maybush, Southampton SO9 4DH.

Prior to commencing any journey by rail, it is advisable to consult the British Rail information office at the relevant London terminus for any time table changes. For telephone numbers see Table 6 (p200).

By careful choice of the day and time of travel it is possible to take advantage of numerous reduced fares offered by British Rail. A free map of the British Rail passenger network is available.

Broadly, it is possible to split the visits into three zones: 1) London and the London and Birmingham Railway; 2) North Wales, Conwy and Llanfairpwll, and 3) Newcastle and Berwick.

London and the London & Birmingham Railway

The following map references are essential:
a) *London A–Z Street Atlas and Index*, (Geographers' A–Z Map Co Ltd)
b) Ordnance Survey Landranger series of Great Britain 1:50000 (about 1¼in to 1 mile or 2cm to 1km)

Table 6 Data on road and rail journeys from London.

From London to	Distance by road Miles	(km)	Principal road route from London	Typical train times	London terminus	Notes
Berwick-on-Tweed	348	(560)	A1(M), A1	3hr 59min	King's Cross	Passenger Service Information 01-278 2477
Birmingham New Street	118	(304)	M1, M6	1hr 31min	Euston	Passenger Service Information 01-387 7070
Chesterfield	148	(238)	M1, A619	2hr 28min	St Pancras	Passenger Service Information 01-387 7070
Chester-le-Street	271	(436)	A1(M), A1, A1(M), A693	—	King's Cross	Change at Newcastle
Conwy	238	(383)	M1, A5, A470	3hr 55min†	Euston	†Via Crewe, Chester to Llandudno junction. Frequent bus service to Conwy
Liverpool Lime Street	210	(338)	M1, M6, M62	2hr 30min	Euston	
Llanfairpwll	248	(399)	M1, A5	4hr 30min†	Euston	†Via Crewe, Chester and Bangor
Manchester Piccadilly	199	(320)	M1, M6, M62	2hr 28min	Euston	
Newcastle	280	(451)	A1(M), A1, A1(M)	3hr 5min	King's Cross	
Rainhill	201	(323)	M1, M6, M62, A57	—	Euston	Change at Liverpool or Manchester. Frequent local service to Rainhill
York	209	(336)	A1(M), A1, A64	1hr 58mins	King's Cross	

Sheet 176 West London
Sheet 165 Aylesbury and Leighton Buzzard
Sheet 152 Northampton and Milton Keynes
Sheet 140 Leicester and Coventry

London

THE SCIENCE MUSEUM (*London A–Z, 62a 2B*)
Exhibition Road, London SW7 2DD (Tel: 01 589 3456)
Nearest tube station: South Kensington (District/Circle/Piccadilly lines)

The Science Museum attracts more visitors than any other museum in London and contains a vast and fascinating range of exhibits demonstrating man's genius and ingenuity. One has to be extremely single-minded to keep to the themes of motive power development and rail transport, but fortuitously these themes are to be found on the ground floor close to the main entrance in Exhibition Road. On entering the museum, the visitor's first view is of the East Hall which contains examples of Newcomen and Watt engines. Proceed through gallery 6 (Exploration) to galleries 7 and 8, Rail Transport. The collection includes the contenders at the Rainhill Trials, the *Rocket, Sans Pareil* and the remains of the *Novelty*. It also has a full-size replica of the *Rocket* as built, sectioned to show internal details. An interesting pamphlet 'The Rocket 1829' may be obtained at the information office which is located at the far end of the East Hall from the main entrance. Galleries 7 and 8 contain numerous exhibits relating to the early development of railways, including a selection of rail sections. The Science Museum library holds a number of the Stephensons' letters (see p175).

Opening hours: weekdays, 10.00–18.00, Sundays 14.30–18.00. Closed all day: New Year's Day, Good Friday, May Day Monday, Christmas Day, Boxing Day. (For other Christmas and Easter arrangements, see press for details.) Admission free during normal opening hours.

THE INSTITUTION OF MECHANICAL ENGINEERS (*London A–Z, 62c, 2D*)
1/3 Birdcage Walk, Westminster, London SW1H 9JJ
Nearest tube stations: Westminster and St James' Park (District/Circle lines).

The institution was founded in 1847 (first president, George Stephenson see p62). The site for its present headquarters was acquired in 1895 and the building was opened in February 1899. The institution made many significant contributions to the advancement of mechanical engineering and the education and training of mechanical engineers. The institution is not generally open to the public.

On entering the building, George Stephenson's influence is immediately apparent with numerous paintings and relics. A solid silver model of the *Rocket* is on display in the library which contains a comprehensive collection of the Stephensons' letters.

THE INSTITUTION OF CIVIL ENGINEERS (*London A–Z*, 62c, 2D)
Great George Street, London SW1H 9JJ
Nearest tube stations: Westminster and St James's Park (District/Circle lines).

The institution was founded in 1818 (first president Thomas Telford) and in 1838 premises were acquired on the opposite side of the road from the present headquarters. The present building was completed in 1913 and contains some impressive rooms, in particular the Great Hall, lecture theatre and main library, all on the first floor.

The influence of Brunel is more apparent than that of the Stephensons, but opposite the bookshop on the ground floor is a large painting of Robert Stephenson and his committee with the Britannia Bridge in the background. The institution is not generally open to the public.

THE ROUND HOUSE (*London A–Z*, 44 2c)
Chalk Farm Road, London NW1
Nearest tube station: Chalk Farm, Northern line, Edgeware branch

The Round House is situated across the road from the tube station and the drab external appearance of Robert Stephenson's engine shed contrasts with the interesting internal structure. The building is lit artificially. Excellent views of the line looking down towards Euston and up towards the entrance to Primrose Hill Tunnel can be obtained from Bridge Approach off Adelaide Road (B509) adjacent to Primrose Hill Station (BR). The east portal of the tunnel is at Primrose Hill Road, off Adelaide Road, about ½ mile (0.8km) from Chalk Farm Station. It is not possible to obtain a clear view of the tunnel entrance as it is obscured by houses and flats.

Between the Round House and Camden Town, Chalk Farm Road crosses the Regent's Canal and access to the towpath is via Commercial Place. Proceed over the hump-back bridge; the bridge carrying the London and Birmingham line over the canal is a short distance along the towpath. Regent's Canal is one of the most interesting amenity water-ways in London and the buildings around Commercial Place have been sensitively restored and contain shops, restaurants, and so on. There is also a busy market at the weekends.

London & Birmingham Railway

It is not practical to inspect the civil engineering works on the line other than by car as the rail option would waste many hours hopping on and off trains and entail long walks. The following route is suggested and can be completed in a day, although careful planning from O/S sheets 176, 165, 152 and 140 is recommended. It includes the following locations: the skew bridge at Hemel Hempstead, Northchurch Tunnel, Tring cutting, Linslade Tunnel, the cast-iron bridge over the A5 at Bletchley, Wolverton embankment and Viaduct, Blisworth/Roade cutting and Kilsby Tunnel. Take the A41 trunk road A41(T) out of London via Hampstead, Hendon, Edgware and Watford (O/S sheet 176). Continue along the A41(T) to Hemel Hempstead. A short distance past the station, the railway crosses the A41 via two skew bridges. The first one, constructed of brick, dates from the opening of the railway and the other from 1875 when the line was duplicated.

Proceed from Hemel Hempstead to Berkhamsted (O/S sheet 165) and at the northern end of the town, turn right at the church on to the B4056, which crosses the canal and then Northchurch Tunnel. Park adjacent to the allotments from which the tunnel portals can be viewed. The original Stephenson portal, wide enough for two tracks, is on the west (canal) side of the line. The length of the tunnel is 367yd (355m). Return to the A41(T) and turn right at the church. Continue for about 2 miles (3.2km) and then take the right-hand fork to Tring Station (1 mile (1.6km)). The Royal Hotel on the right at the approach to Tring Station dates from the opening of the railway and its courtyard and stables have recently been restored. Cross the railway bridge which is at the south end of the cutting and turn left. Follow the road for about half the length of the cutting and then turn left on to the B488. From Folly Bridge there is an impressive view of the cutting, although it is marred by the galaxy of galvanised steel structures associated with overhead electrification. At this point the depth of the cutting is about 60ft (18m) deep — note the steep slopes excavated in the chalk.

Follow the B488 towards Ivinghoe, bear left noting the Pitstone Windmill (National Trust) with the cement works in the background.

Proceed through the village and turn right at the church of St Mary the Virgin and continue along the B488 with the railway to the left. At the approaches to Linslade bear right at the 'Picture Gallery' on to the Leighton Buzzard–Aylesbury road (A418). Turn left on to the A4146 at the mini-roundabout (Bedford Arms facing). At the second mini-roundabout take the Stoke Hammond road (A4146) and a short distance outside Linslade a tunnel shaft can be seen on the hill to the left. The A418 crosses the railway a short distance from the north portal to Linslade Tunnel (284yd (260m)). There are three tunnels of which the central tunnel carrying two tracks is the original, opened in 1837. The outer two tunnels were opened in 1859 and 1876. The portals have interesting castellated and turreted embellishments. From Linslade Tunnel continue along the A4146 passing the Three Locks public house on the right and proceed through Stoke Hammond. At the approaches to Bletchley, turn right at the first mini-roundabout and straight over the second and third mini-roundabouts and continue into Fenny Stratford. At the multi-mini-roundabout turn left (signpost Denbigh and Bletchley, MK1). Refer to O/S sheet 152 noting that this is the original route of the A5 (Watling Street). Fenny Stratford Station is signposted on the right and continue over the next roundabout (Milton Keynes North, A5). A short distance past the roundabout, the railway crosses the A5 via a skew bridge. On the north side, the original cast-iron structure has been preserved (the beams are painted yellow), but it is no longer in use. Although the A5 has been by-passed by the A5(T) at Bletchley, it is still a busy road and parking in a side road on the right to the north of the cast-iron bridge is recommended.

Continue north along the A5 and at the approaches to Stony Stratford a roundabout forms the start of the ring road. There are two options here: take the ring road and then bear right into Wolverton or negotiate the dog leg and proceed straight into Stony Stratford. The Cock Inn, which is reputed to have been used by Robert Stephenson, is on the A5 in the centre of the town. If the latter option is taken, leave Stony Stratford via the Wolverton road at the Plough Inn. The bus station is about 100yd (91m) down the Wolverton road on the right. Proceed straight across the roundabout under the A5(T) and continue into Wolverton passing British Rail Engineering Works Ltd on the left. Cross the bridge and pass straight over the mini-roundabout (signpost to Castlethorpe) with the railway embankment on the left. A short distance along this road there is a picnic and parking area on the left. It is possible to walk under the viaduct which crosses the River Great

Ouse. The joint separating the original and duplicate viaduct may be clearly seen. The original viaduct is on the east side. It is not as elegant as Brunel's viaduct at Hanwell which was built in the same period. Nevertheless, Robert Stephenson's viaduct has considerable visual impact.

Return through Wolverton on the same route (station and engineering works on the right). Pass under the A5(T) and turn immediately right on to the ring road. Turn right again at the junction with the A5 (Watling Street) and at the next roundabout, take the second exit on to the A508 (Northampton Road). Proceed through Yardley Gobion to the signpost, Stoke Bruerne ½ mile (0.8m).

Here a brief diversion from railway interests is recommended to visit the Canal Waterways Museum and the south portal of William Jessop's Blisworth Tunnel (3,076yd (2,812m)). For the museum opening times telephone Northampton (0604) 862229. Provided an early morning start has been made, Stoke Bruerne is a convenient stopping place (use museum car park) and apart from the museum and shop, there are some interesting canalside cottages, restaurants and a pub, the old Boat Inn. The south portal of the canal tunnel is a few hundred yards north of the museum. The tunnel is currently closed as extensive repair work is underway.

Departing from the museum car park, cross over the canal bridge and turn right on to the Blisworth road. A short distance north of Stoke Bruerne, this road crosses the disused Stratford-upon-Avon & Midland Junction Railway which was opened in 1891. Stoke Bruerne Station can be seen on the left. The road follows the line of the canal tunnel (note the ventilation shafts) into Blisworth. Turn right on to the A43(T) and then right again on to the minor road which links the A43(T) and the A508. Travelling towards Roade, the most spectacular views on the whole of the length of the London & Birmingham Railway can be obtained from the bridge which carries the road over Roade cutting. From the north parapet, the main line to Rugby and Birmingham may be seen forking to the left and the Northampton loop to the right. The loop from Roade through Northampton and Long Buckby to Rugby was opened in 1882. The original branch to Northampton, opened in 1845, commenced at the Blisworth Hotel (Blisworth Station no longer exists) which is about 2 miles (3.2km) along the London and Birmingham line from the bridge over Roade cutting. The original Stephenson portion of this bridge is best viewed from a path which runs along the top of the east slope of the cutting. Access to the path is via a wooden gate with a notice about the dangers of overhead live wires. Looking south from the bridge parapet along the deep cutting towards Roade, the extent of the excavations, which were carried out between 1834 and 1838 by thousands of navvies, make their reputed average daily consumption of 2lb (1kg) of meat, 2lb (1kg) of bread and 5qt (5 litres) of ale quite credible (T. Coleman), along with the extended 'randies'.

The final major location, Kilsby Tunnel is reached via the following route. From the bridge over Roade cutting, travel east and turn left on to the A508, Turn left again on to the M1 (Junction 15). Proceed along the M1 to Junction 18 (O/S sheet 140) and leave the motorway following the A428 (A5) towards Rugby. At the traffic lights, turn left on to the A5(T), signposted to Milton Keynes (Kilsby 1¼ miles (2km)). The A5(T) crosses the northern end of the Northampton loop and a short distance on, it crosses the London and Birmingham line; the north portal of Kilsby Tunnel can be seen on the left.

At Kilsby the A5(T) bears left and crosses the line of the tunnel. A massive castellated ventilation shaft can be seen on the left, a few yards from the road (Plate 81). The remaining access shafts are now seen on the right-hand side of the road with the second castellated ventilation shaft in the distance. Immediately after crossing over the M45, turn sharp right (signposted to Ashby St Ledgers, 1½ miles [2.4km] gated road) and a short distance on, the road crosses the line over the south portal of the tunnel. A short distance on, there is an access gate to a path

Plate 81 The Kilsby Tunnel ventilation shaft close to the A5 trunk road, the most symbolic landmark on the London & Birmingham Railway (*Derrick Beckett*)

which leads along the cutting from which the portal can be observed.

For the return journey (O/S sheet 152), proceed through the picturesque village of Ashby St Ledgers, turn right at the church then left and left again, on to the road leading to the village of Watford. Continue along this road for about 1½ miles (2.4km), turn left on to the B4036 and then right on to the A5(T) travelling south. The A5(T) runs parallel to the canal, railway and M1 motorway and they are in close proximity at Watford Gap, Long Buckby Wharf and Whilton locks. At Weedon Bec turn left on to the A45(T) which joins the M1 at Junction 16. Continue south to London.

North Wales — Conwy and Britannia Bridges

The return journey to North Wales by car or train to inspect the Conwy and Britannia tubular bridges requires half a day's travelling by train or car in each direction and thus it is preferable to allow three days for the visit. A two-day visit by car is possible, but it allows little time to take in the numerous scenic and architectural attractions of North Wales. *A Glimpse of the Past*, published by the Wales Tourist Board, is a useful guide to the industrial architecture of Wales and lists the principal tourist information centres. Regional head office: North Wales Tourism Council, Glam-y-don Hall, Civic Centre, Colwyn Bay, Clwyd. Tel: Colwyn Bay (0492) 56881. See also *Where to stay in Wales* (70p) from Welsh Tourist Board, PO Box 1, Cardiff CF1 2XN.

The Route by Road
The journey by road offers the traveller greater flexibility than the train. Take the M1 out of London and join the A5 at junction 18. The A5 runs to the north of Birmingham and Wolverhampton (alternatively join the M6 at junction 19 which links with the A5 at junction 12). The M54 (see O/S Route Planner) is not as yet (1982) completed, but the completed section skirts the southern outskirts of Telford. West of Shrewsbury there are a number of examples of Telford's feats of bridge and aqueduct construction — Chirk Aqueduct (1801) can be seen to the west of the A5 at the junction with the B4500 to Glyn Ceiriog (O/S sheet 126) and the Pontcysylte Aqueduct (1794–1805) is off the A5 near Trefor (O/S sheet 117) between Chirk and Llangollen. At Betws-y-Coed (O/S sheet 115), the A5 crosses Waterloo Bridge, designed by Telford and constructed in 1816. This is a graceful cast-iron arch with extensive decoration. Proceed along the A5 from Betws-y-Coed and

here the superb alignment of Telford's road can be fully appreciated as it winds its way along the valley with the mountains rising to in excess of 3,000ft (1,000m). At Bangor (O/S sheet 115), follow the A5 through the town. The A5 crosses the Menai Strait via Telford's suspension bridge (1826). Turn left on the Anglesey side and continue to Llanfairpwll (LLANFAIRPWLLGWYNGLLGOGERYCHWYMDROBWLLIANTYSILIOGOGOGOCH) past the approaches to the Britannia Bridge. Turn left at the Carreg Bran Country Hotel into Church Lane and it is possible to park close to St Mary's Church. There is a fine view of the Britannia Bridge from the parking area, but this is enhanced by a walk through the graveyard to the shore. Tide permitting, walk across the foreshore to Nelson's statue (Clarence Paget, 1873) and view the bridge from the observation platform. The iron steps within the statue are a little precarious. For a closer inspection, return to the A5 and cross the bridge and on the Caernarvon shore, turn left into an access road which passes under the bridge approaches where there is parking space. Here the scale of the lions guarding the approaches to the original bridge can be appreciated. A section of the tube has been preserved and stands close to the bridge. Note the thickness of the plates and the number of rivets required in a 6ft (1.8m) length.

There is a model of the Britannia Bridge at the Marquis of Anglesey's home, Plas Newydd, Llandairpwll, Gwynedd, which is now owned by the National Trust and overlooks the Menai Strait.

The Museum of Welsh Antiquities, Tford Gwynedd, Bangor LL57 1DT (Tel: Bangor [0248] 51151) has extensive material on the Menai bridges, including a number of lithographs, engravings and photographs and in particular, G. Hawkin's lithographs depicting the Britannia Bridge in various stages of construction.

To continue the journey to Conwy, take the A55 North Wales coast road out of Bangor which follows the railway line for about 16 miles (26km) to Conwy. Between Penmaenmawr and the Penmaenbach headland there is a tunnel under the sea wall carrying Stephenson's railway (close to the youth hostel). From the foreshore there is a panoramic view of the sea wall and the headland. At Conwy, the tubular bridge is alongside Telford's suspension bridge and the A55 is carried across the River Conwy on a later arched bridge. The bridges are dwarfed by the castle from which one can look down on the three structures crossing the river, shortly to be paralleled by a fourth, an immersed tube tunnel carrying the A55 under the Conwy estuary.

The Route by Rail

An early morning train from Euston arrives at Llandudno about mid-day. Llandudno Junction is about 1 mile (1.6km) from Conwy and there is a frequent bus service with a journey time of about five minutes. Use Llandudno Junction Station as the starting point for the journey to the Britannia Bridge. The train passenger is rewarded by more leisurely views of the coastline and on crossing the Britannia Bridge, look along the strait towards Bangor to see Telford's suspension bridge. Alight at Llanfairpwll — the bridge is at a short walk from the station. An additional attraction on the outskirts of the village is the Marquess of Anglesey's column, 112ft (34m) high; a spiral staircase leads to a gallery beneath the statue (open daily).

Newcastle and Berwick

The following maps are useful:
a) *Newcastle-upon-Tyne A–Z Street Atlas and Index* (Geographers' A–Z Map Co Ltd)
b) *A–Z Newcastle-upon-Tyne Premier Street Map* with index of streets (Geographers' A–Z Map Co Ltd)
c) O/S Sheet 88, Newcastle-upon-Tyne

A limited day trip to Newcastle by train is possible — a typical HST125 journey time from King's Cross to Newcastle is just over three hours. The fastest time is the Flying Scotsman, 2hr 54min, but it leaves too late in the morning. An earlier train is recommended to allow five hours to take in the High Level Bridge, the Literary and Philosophical Society building, the statue of George Stephenson (both close to the station) and the site of the Forth Street locomotive works. An Act of Parliament for the building of Central Station, Newcastle, was sanctioned in 1845 and the 600ft (183m) long curved arched train shed was completed in 1850 (architect John Dobson). There have been several extensions and the Royal Station Hotel was completed in the 1890s.

They are all located within map reference 60 3c, *Newcastle-upon-Tyne A–Z*. Newcastle and its environs has formed such an important role in the birth and development of railways that it warrants extending the day visit to three or four days and hiring a car at Newcastle.

There is a city information service and tourist information centre at the central library, Newcastle-upon-Tyne NE99 1MC (Tel: Newcastle [0632] 611348). The British Rail information office is at Central Station

Plate 82 The statue of George Stephenson in Newcastle-upon-Tyne (*Frances Gibson-Smith*)

Plate 83 The site of the Forth Street locomotive works in Newcastle-upon-Tyne, the headquarters of Robert Stephenson & Co *(Frances Gibson-Smith)*

(Tel: Newcastle [0632] 326262). The following itinerary is suggested, using public transport for locations near the centre of the city as the road system is complex and it is convenient to book a hotel close to the station.

DAY 1 AM — High Level Bridge, Literary and Philosophical Society, George Stephenson's statue, Forth Street locomotive works

PM — Take Tyne Valley line from Newcastle Central Station (frequent service) to Wylam, about ten minutes. Cross over the road bridge and turn right following the track alongside the river in an easterly direction. Stephenson's cottage is a few minutes' walk opposite a picnic area.

DAY 2 (car) — A day trip to Berwick via Dial Cottage at Killingworth. Use *A–Z Premier Street Map* to locate Dial Cottage. From central Newcastle take the A6125 to junction with A189 at West Jesmond. Take third exit into Jesmond Dene Road and follow the A189 via Killingworth Road and Salters Lane to the roundabout at the junction with the A188. Take the second exit into Benton Lane and then turn right into Great Lime Road (B1318). Dial Cottage is a short

211

distance along the road on the left-hand side. To proceed to Berwick-upon-Tweed, continue along the B1318 and turn left into Whitley Road (A186) and then the A1 at the interchange. Proceed along the A1 to Berwick, about 60 miles (96km). The Tweed Bridge, about ⅓ mile (0.5km) downstream from Stephenson's Royal Border Bridge, carries the A1 over the River Tweed into Golden Square. At the top of Golden Square, turn left into Castlegate. There is a tourist information centre on the right-hand side at Castlegate car park (Tel: Berwick [0289] 7187). Do not park at Castlegate but at the car park close to the station and Castle Dene Park. Walk down through the park to the river walkway, which passes under the arches of the Royal Border Bridge. The English Tourist Board mini-guide to Berwick-upon-Tweed (10p) can be obtained from the information centre.

As an alternative, take the High Speed Train from Central Station, Newcastle, to Berwick, journey time about one hour. The nearest metro station to Dial Cottage is at Benton. Walk up Station Road and Forest Hall Road and turn left into Great Lime Road and Dial Cottage is on the right (a 1 mile (1.6km) walk from Benton metro).

DAY 3 (car) — There is a difficult choice of railway museums and the reader is left to decide. At Shildon there is Timothy Hackworth's Cottage Museum which incorporates a rail trail covering much of the original route of the Stockton & Darlington Railway, including Brusselton incline. Take the A1(M) travelling about 30 miles (48.2km) south from Newcastle and turn right on to the A68 in the direction of West Auckland and Consett. Proceed along the A68 for about 2 miles (3.2km) and take the right fork (A6072) to Shildon.

The North Road Museum at Darlington is devoted to the history of the Stockton & Darlington Railway and the North Eastern Railway. The station dates from 1842 and the exhibits include the original locomotion of 1825. Route as for Shildon but turn left on to the A68 and proceed into Darlington.

The largest museum is the North of England Open Air Museum, Beamish Hall, Stanley (Tel: Stanley [0207] 31811). It is a regional museum administered by a consortium of four county councils and occupies the Beamish Hall Estate covering about 200 acres (80ha). This is an ambitious project and includes a railway station, using the rebuilt Rowley Station (1867) and various ancillary structures, a projected town, pit cottages and a colliery. Associated with the colliery is a working replica of *Locomotion* (Plate 10) made by local engineering firms for the 150th anniversary of the Stockton & Darlington Railway. Check with museum for steaming times.

Two additional visits are to the National Railway Museum, York and Tapton House and Holy Trinity Church, Chesterfield.

York

THE NATIONAL RAILWAY MUSEUM, Leeman Road, York YO2 4XJ (Tel: York [0904] 21261).

Advantage can be taken of the HST125 train service from King's Cross to York (about two hours) for a one-day trip, which allows about six hours to visit the museum, but no time for a tour of the walled city and York Minster. The arched roof of York Station (Thomas Prosser, 1877), built on a curve, is one of the finest examples of Victorian station architecture and recent redecoration enhances its appearance. The museum is about ten minutes' walk from the station (follow the signposts) and an important exhibit, the Gaunless Bridge, is outside the museum alongside the car park. George Stephenson's statue, rescued from the Great Hall at Euston Station, is close to the entrance to the main hall.

Apart from the superb collection of some of the world's most evocative locomotives, including the *Mallard* and a working replica of the *Rocket*, there are numerous other exhibits relating to early railway development. These include the Swannington incline winding engine and short sections of track — Blenkinsop, Stephenson and Brunel.

Opening hours: weekdays 10.00–18.00, Sundays 14.30–18.00. Closed all day: New Year's Day, Good Friday, May Day Bank Holiday, Christmas Eve, Christmas Day, Boxing Day. (For other Christmas/New Year arrangements, see press for details.) Admission free during opening hours.

Chesterfield

TAPTON HOUSE AND HOLY TRINITY CHURCH

A possible diversion on route by road to York or Newcastle (take the M1 rather than the A1 route out of London). Leave the M1 at junction 30 (O/S sheet 140) and take the A619 into Chesterfield via Stavely. Tapton House, now a comprehensive school, is on the left-hand side of the hill leading down to Chesterfield and situated in 30 acres (12ha) of public park. At the bottom of the hill is George Stephenson's line from Derby to Sheffield. Holy Trinity Church, not to be confused with Chesterfield's most famous landmark, the church with the crooked spire, is close to the centre of the town.

TECHNICAL APPENDICES

I Structural Mechanics

It is possible to make an approximate quantitative assessment of bridges designed by Robert Stephenson with the assistance of others, in particular, William Fairbairn and Eaton Hodgkinson. This assessment generally relies on the use of structural mechanics at the level known at the date of construction of the bridges. The formulae applied are stated below:

The maximum bending moment in a simply supported beam, of span L and subjected to a total uniformly distributed load W, is given by

$$M = 0.125 \, WL \quad \text{(equation 1)}$$

The deflection of a simply supported beam subjected to a total uniformly distributed load W and span L is given

by

$$M = \frac{WL^3}{77EI} \quad \text{(equation 2)}$$

where
$$E = \text{modulus of elasticity}$$
$$I = \text{second moment of area}$$

The stress f at a distance y from the neutral axis of a beam section of second moment of area I and subjected to a bending moment M, is given by

$$f = \frac{My}{I} \quad \text{(equation 3)}$$

The horizontal thrust H in a parabolic arch of span L, rise h and subjected to a total uniformly distributed load W is given by

$$H = \frac{WL}{8h} \quad \text{(equation 4)}$$

II The Dee Bridge

In Chapter 5 reference was made to the use of Hodgkinson's formula ($W = \frac{26\,A_b\,d}{L}$) for estimating the proportions of cast-iron girders. The proportions of the Dee Bridge girders, drawn to scale and ignoring mouldings, are shown in Fig 54 and the slenderness of the top (compression) flange is immediately apparent. The section properties are evaluated below:

Location of neutral axis:

$$
\begin{aligned}
\text{area} \quad = \quad & 24 \times 2.5 & = & \quad 60 \\
& 41 \times 2.125 & = & \quad 87.125 \\
& 7.5 \times 1.5 & = & \quad \underline{11.25} \\
& & & \quad 158.375\,\text{in}^2\,(102 \times 10^3\text{mm}^2)
\end{aligned}
$$

The distance of the neutral axis from the bottom fibre is given by

$$
= \quad \frac{60 \times 1.25 + 87.125 \times 23 + 11.25 \times 44.25}{158.375}
$$

$$
= \quad 16.27\text{in}\,(413\text{mm})
$$

$$
d - 16.27 \quad = \quad 28.73\text{in}\,(730\text{mm})
$$

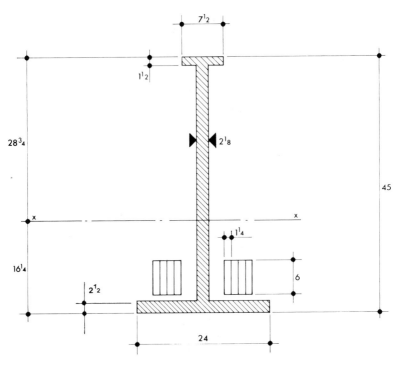

Fig 54 Dimensions of the Dee Bridge cast-iron girders

Second moment of area about neutral axis:

$$
\begin{array}{lcr}
0.083 \times 24 \times 2.5^3 & = & 31.35 \\
60 \times 15.02^2 & = & 13536.02 \\
0.083 \times 2.125 \times 41^3 & = & 12204.76 \\
87.125 \times 6.73^2 & = & 3946.14 \\
0.083 \times 7.5 \times 1.5^3 & = & 2.11 \\
11.25 \times 27.98^2 & = & 8807.40 \\
\hline
Ix & = & 38527.78 \text{in}^4\,(1.6 \times 10^{10}\text{mm}^4)
\end{array}
$$

First moment of area about neutral axis:

$$
\begin{array}{lcr}
11.25 \times 27.98 & = & 314.77 \\
12.57.86 \times 13.615 & = & 787.64 \\
\hline
& & 1102.41\text{in}^3\,(18.06 \times 10^6\text{mm}^3)
\end{array}
$$

The design load for the girder considered as a static uniformly distributed load is in the order of 0.8 ton/ft.

The maximum bending moment for an effective span of 103.5ft is given by

$$
\begin{aligned}
M & = 0.125 \times 0.8 \times 103.5^2 \\
& = 1071.2 \text{ tons ft}\,(3{,}296\text{kNm})
\end{aligned}
$$

The corresponding stresses are

$$
\begin{aligned}
f \text{ top} & = \frac{1071.2 \times 12 \times 28.73}{38527.78} \\
& = 9.58 \text{ tons/in}^2 \text{ compression}\,(148\text{N/mm}^2)
\end{aligned}
$$

$$
\begin{aligned}
f \text{ btm} & = \frac{1071.2 \times 12 \times 16.27}{38527.78} \\
& = 5.43 \text{ tons/in}^2 \text{ tension}\,(83.9\text{N/mm}^2)
\end{aligned}
$$

The maximum shear force

$$
\begin{aligned}
& = 0.8 \times 103.5 \times 0.5 \\
& = 41.4 \text{ tons}\,(414\text{kN})
\end{aligned}
$$

and the corresponding shear stress at the neutral axis is

$$
\begin{aligned}
& = \frac{41.4 \times 1102.41}{38527.78 \times 2.125} \\
& = 0.55 \text{ tons/in}^2\,(8.5\text{N/mm}^2)
\end{aligned}
$$

The average shear stress on a web area 41 x 2.125in is

$$= \frac{41.4}{41 \times 2.125}$$
$$= 0.475 \text{ tons/in}^2 \ (7.34^\text{N}/\text{mm}^2)$$

A typical average value for the ultimate tensile strength of cast iron is 7 tons/in^2(108$^\text{N}$/mm^2) and thus the margin of safety against failure of the tension flange is small. The provision of wrought-iron ties increased the tension flange area by 60in^2(387cm^2), but unfortunately composite action was not achieved and the eccentricity of the ties at the ends of the girders (see Fig 30) induced additional compression in the top flange. The cause of failure can be attributed to the girder deflecting sideways and buckling. It is not possible to quantify this mode of failure by the application of structural mechanics and a theoretical treatment of the problem was not available until the beginning of the twentieth century (Timoshenko). From the differential equation for lateral buckling, it is possible to derive an expression for the buckling load which is related to the torsional and warping rigidities of the girder, the type of loading and the position of application of the load, which for the Dee Bridge was on the bottom flange. It is estimated that the buckling load is in the range 90 tons (concentrated load at midspan) to 140 tons (uniformly distributed load). For the Dee Bridge the real loading conditions are represented by a uniformly distributed load and a series of concentrated loads. Thus the buckling load could lie within the range 90 to 140 tons (900 to 1,400kN).

However, no account is taken of initial twist resulting from the mode of application of the load to the bottom flange or the initial lack of straightness of the girder. This leads to the conclusion that the buckling load may be less than the design load of about 82 tons (820kN). Stephenson's test result (see p129) justifies this conclusion.

III The Britannia and Conwy Tubular Bridges

Fairbairn carried out a test to obtain the crushing strength of a square tube of similar proportions to those used for the Britannia and Conwy bridges. An 18in (450mm) sq tube 8ft (2.4m) long was fabricated in the form shown in Fig 55 from 1/2in (12.5mm) plate. The plates were riveted to 4in x 4in x 1/2in (100mm x 100mm x 12.5mm) angles, but the spacing of the rivets was not stated. The tube was placed vertically under a hydraulic press and failed at a load of about 680 tons (6800kN). Thus the average compressive stress at failure was 680/50 = 13.6 tons/in^2 (210$^\text{N}$/mm^2). This stress is significantly below the Euler stress for the tube as a whole and the local plate buckling stress. However, it will be shown that the stresses in the Britannia and Conwy tubes under full design load are at a level at which there is an adequate margin of safety against failure. Flat plates from ironworks in Yorkshire, Shropshire, Derbyshire and Staffordshire were also subjected to tension tests, the material being extended in a direction parallel and perpendicular to the fibres. There was no significant difference in

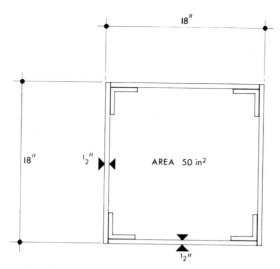

Fig 55 Square tube tested by William Fairbairn

the stress at failure which averaged about 22.75 tons/in^2 (352N/mm^2). This work was extended to double and single riveted joints and the relative strength of the plates alone to that of the double and single riveted joints was approximately 100:70:56.

Dimensions of the Tube
The overall dimensions of the tubes are given on p138, and Plates 84 and 85 illustrate the arrangement of the plates in the longitudinal and transverse direction. The plates for the 1ft 9in (525mm) top cells (Plate 84) are all 6ft (1,800mm) long varying in thickness from ¾in (19mm) at the centre to ⅝in (16mm) at the ends of the tubes. The plates for the 2ft 4in (711mm) bottom cells are all 12ft (3,600mm) long varying in thickness from ⁹/₁₆in (14mm) at the centre to ⁷/₁₆in (10mm) at the ends. The vertical plates are 2ft (610mm) wide and alternately 6ft 6in (1,950mm) and 8ft 8in (2,600mm) long (see Plate 84) and are ½in (12.5mm) thick at the centre and ⅝in (16mm) thick at the ends. This is a logical arrangement as the vertical plates resist shear, which is at a maximum at the ends of the tubes, whereas the cells resist the tension and compression due to bending, which is at a maximum at midspan, if the beam is simply supported. The major problem was the fabrication of the tubes from plates of relatively small dimensions. A 12ft x 2ft 4in (3,600mm x 700mm) plate was at the upper limit of the size that could be rolled, and prior to connecting the plates it was necessary to flatten them with large hammers. The fabrication of the Britannia tubes required upwards of 1.75 million 1in (25mm) diameter rivets and an even larger number of holes to be punched in the plates. Punching of the holes was greatly facilitated by Richard Roberts (1789–1864), a machine maker and inventor, who devised a machine for punching holes at precise intervals in wrought-iron plates. The plates for the sides and cells were connected by flats, L- and T-sections. The rivet spacing for the horizontal plates was 4in (102mm) and 3in (76mm) for the vertical plates. As indicated in

219

Plate 84 The top cells of the preserved section of a Britannia Bridge tube (*Frances Gibson-Smith*)

Plate 85 A corner of the bottom cell of the tube (*Frances Gibson-Smith*)

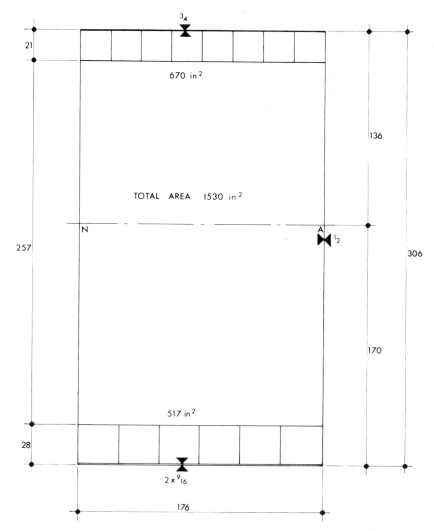

$^3_4$

21

670 in^2

136

TOTAL AREA 1530 in^2

N

257

A

$^1_2$

306

170

517 in^2

28

$2 \times {}^9_{16}$

176

Fig 56 Approximate dimensions of the Conwy tube at midspan

Chapter 6 the rivets were placed by hand and the rivet head was formed by hammering a steel cup-shaped tool on the previously heated metal.

Approximate Analysis of the Tubes

The principal dimensions of the Conwy tube at midspan are shown in Fig 56. These are based on Fairbairn's report. The section properties are estimated as follows:

$$
\begin{array}{lll}
\text{area of top cells} & = & 670\text{in}^2\,(0.432 \times 10^6\text{mm}^2) \\
\text{area of bottom cells} & = & 517\text{in}^2\,(0.333 \times 10^6\text{mm}^2) \\
\text{total area} & = & 1{,}530\text{in}^2\,(0.986 \times 10^6\text{mm}^2)
\end{array}
$$

Thus it can be deduced that the area of the side plates (webs) is 343in² (0.221 x 10⁶mm²). Referring to Fig 56 it would appear that the area of the side plates is 257in² (2 x 257 x 0.5). Examination of Fairbairn's report leads to the conclusion that his figures cannot necessarily be taken as entirely reliable and the analysis below uses the more conservative web area of 257in² (0.166 x 10⁶mm²).

Depth of neutral axis:

$$
\begin{array}{rcl}
670 \times (306 - 10.5) & = & 197{,}985 \\
517 \times 14 & = & 7{,}238 \\
257 \times (128.5 + 28) & = & 40{,}220 \\
\hline
1{,}444 & & 245{,}443
\end{array}
$$

$$
\begin{array}{rcl}
\text{Thus depth of neutral axis} & = & \dfrac{245{,}443}{1{,}444} \\
 & = & 170\text{in}\,(4.32\text{m})\text{ from bottom}
\end{array}
$$

Second moment of area I

$$
\begin{array}{rcl}
670 \times (136 - 10.5)^2 & = & 10{,}552{,}667 \\
517 \times (170 - 14)^2 & = & 12{,}581{,}712 \\
0.083 \times 257^3 & = & 1{,}414{,}549 \\
257 \times 13.5^2 & = & 46{,}838 \\
\text{Thus I} & = & 24{,}595{,}766\text{in}^4\,(1.02 \times 10^{13}\text{mm}^4)
\end{array}
$$

Fairbairn quotes an I value of 17.9 x 10⁶in⁴. The higher value of 24.6 x 10⁶in⁴ will be used to estimate the stresses and deflections. The total weight of the Conwy tube is given as 1,300 tons which includes lifting frames. The clear span is 400ft with an overall length of 424ft. Using an effective span of 412ft, the maximum bending moment is given by

$$
\begin{array}{rcl}
M & = & 0.125 \times 1300 \times 412 \\
 & = & 66{,}950\text{ ton ft}\,(2.06 \times 10^5\text{kNm})
\end{array}
$$

$$
\begin{array}{rcl}
\text{Thus top fibre stress} & = & \dfrac{66950 \times 12 \times 136}{24.6 \times 10^6} \\
 & = & 4.44\text{ tons/in}^2\,(68.6^\text{N}/\text{mm}^2)\text{ compression}
\end{array}
$$

$$
\begin{array}{rcl}
\text{Bottom fibre stress} & = & \dfrac{66950 \times 12 \times 170}{24.6 \times 10^6} \\
 & = & 5.55\text{ tons/in}^2\,(85.7^\text{N}/\text{mm}^2)\text{ tension}
\end{array}
$$

Assuming a train load of about 1 ton per foot (32.5kN/m) run, the total additional load is 412 tons (4,120kN) resulting in additional compression and tension stresses of 1.44 tons/in² (22.3ᴺ/mm²) and 1.8 tons/in² (27.8ᴺ/mm²) respectively. Thus the maximum stresses are

$$\text{Compression} \quad = \quad 4.44 + 1.44 \quad = \quad 5.88 \text{ tons/in}^2 \,(90.1\text{N/mm}^2)$$
$$\text{Tension} \qquad\quad = \quad 5.55 + 1.80 \quad = \quad 7.35 \text{ tons/in}^2 \,(113.5\text{N/mm}^2)$$

Using Fairbairn's test value of 13.6 tons/in² (210N/mm²) at failure (single-tube test), the stress margin of safety is 13.6/5.88 = 2.31.

The deflection of the tube under a load of 1,300 tons is
$$= \quad \frac{1300 \times 2240 \times 1728 \times 412^3}{.77 \times 24.6 \times 10^6 \times 28 \times 10^6}$$
$$= \quad 6.63\text{in}\,(168.4\text{mm})$$

Fairbairn measured the deflection of the Conwy tube resting between supports as 7.91in (201mm). In the above calculation the modulus of elasticity of wrought iron was taken as 28.0 x 10⁶lb/in² (194kN/mm²), which may be rather high for the grade of material used in 1845–50.

The average shear stress in the webs, ⅝in thick at the supports is
$$= \quad \frac{1300 \times 0.5}{257 \times 0.625 \times 2}$$
$$= \quad 2.02 \text{ tons/in}^2\,(31.2\text{N/mm}^2)$$

Plate 86 Part of a Conwy tube showing the vertical T-sections at 24in (61cm) intervals which stiffen the web plates (*Frances Gibson-Smith*)

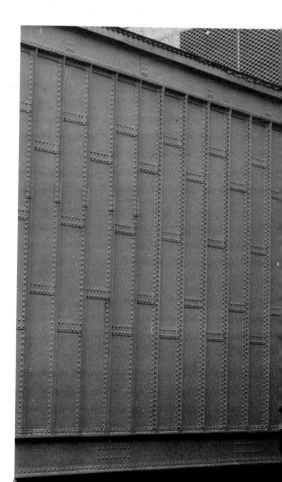

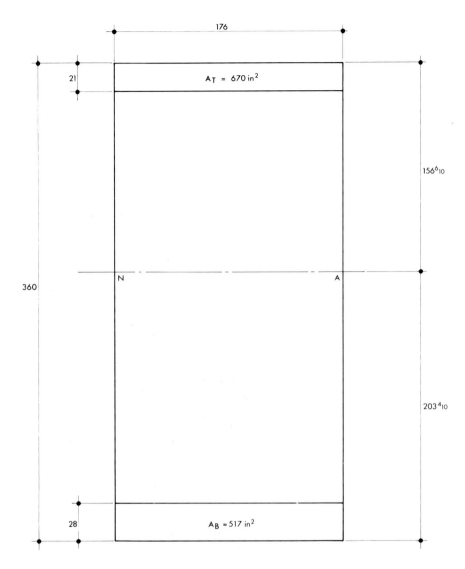

Fig 57 Approximate dimensions of a Britannia tube at the centre of a 460ft (140m) span

The web plates were stiffened by T-sections at 24in (61cm) intervals (see Plate 86).

The above, albeit simple calculations, demonstrate in general terms the adequacy of the tubes to carry their self-weight plus the train load without the assistance of suspension chains.

The sequence of construction for the Britannia tubes can be described as subtle. Firstly, an estimate of the section properties of the Britannia tube at the centre of the 460ft (141.5m) main span can be made with sufficient accuracy using Fig 57. From the previous calculation for the Conwy Bridge, it can be

224

seen that the contribution of the webs to the second moment of area I, is small. Thus the analysis will proceed on the basis that the cellular top and bottom flanges carry the bending and the webs the shear. Location of neutral axis:

$$
\begin{array}{lcl}
670 \times (360 - 10.5) & = & 234{,}165 \\
\underline{517 \times 14} & = & \underline{7{,}238} \\
1{,}187 & = & 241{,}403
\end{array}
$$

$$
\begin{array}{lcl}
\text{Thus depth of neutral axis} & = & \dfrac{241{,}403}{1{,}187} \\
 & = & 203.4\text{in} \ (5.16\text{m}) \text{ from bottom}
\end{array}
$$

Second moment of area I
$$
\begin{array}{lcl}
670 \times (156.6 - 10.5)^2 & = & 14{,}301{,}290 \\
517 \times (203.4 - 14)^2 & = & 18{,}546{,}010 \\
 & & 32{,}847{,}300\text{in}^4 \ (13.67 \times 10^{12}\text{mm}^4)
\end{array}
$$

Using a value of, say, $32.5 \times 10^6 \text{in}^4$, the bending moment and stresses at the centre of a main tube under an estimated total load of 1,600 tons (16,000kN), uniformly distributed over a simply supported span of 460ft (141.5m) are:

$$
\begin{array}{lcl}
\text{Moment} & = & 1{,}600 \times 460 \times 0.125 \\
 & = & 92{,}000 \text{ tons ft} \ (283{,}076\text{kNm}) \\
\text{Stresses} & = & \dfrac{92000 \times 156.6 \times 12}{32.5 \times 10^6} \\
 & = & 5.32 \text{ tons/in}^2 \ (82.2^{\text{N}}/\text{mm}^2) \text{ compression} \\
 & = & \dfrac{92000 \times 203.4 \times 12}{32.5 \times 10^6} \\
 & = & 6.91 \text{ tons/in}^2 \ (106.8^{\text{N}}/\text{mm}^2) \text{ tension}
\end{array}
$$

At this stage a main tube BC rests between the two piers. The second main tube CD was then raised into position from the pontoons (see Chapter 6) and the outer 230ft (71m) spans BA and DE had been previously constructed on timber staging. Assuming a total uniformly distributed load for all tubes of 1,600/460, approximately 3.5 tons per foot (114kN/m) run, the midspan bending moments for the tubes simply supported between the piers and abutments are shown on Fig 58a. The moments in spans AB and DE would only occur with the staging lowered. If the four tubes had been erected on staging and made continuous at the joints, and the staging lowered, the resulting moments would be as Fig 58b. This gives a more favourable distribution of moments throughout the structure but it was not practical to construct the bridge in this way owing to navigation requirements. To obtain a more even distribution of moment, tubes AB and DE were connected to BC and CD at a tilt (see Fig 58c). On lowering the tubes to the horizontal, a moment M was induced at B and E. Thus the advantage of continuity for the self-weight of the

225

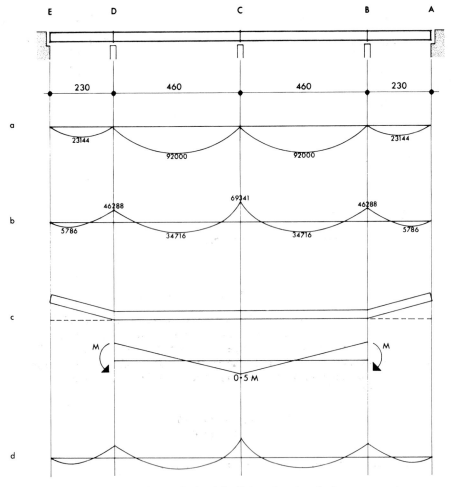

Fig 58 A simplified analysis of the Britannia tubes during construction

structure and for subsequent train loads was effected with a bending moment distribution of the form shown in Fig 58d.

It must be noted that the continuous beam bending moment distribution results in compressive stresses being induced in the bottom cells of the tubes, the proportions of which were originally developed from considerations of tension. To summarise, the member and section analysis of the Britannia Bridge was broadly within the limits of current theoretical knowledge. It is almost certain that a design based on calculations alone would have resulted in possible failure owing to instability of the webs or compression flanges. Further, the tests on the riveted joints were essential considering the importance of the joint design to the strength of a structure fabricated from a series of small plates to span 460ft (140m).

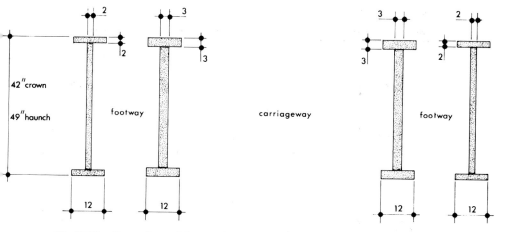

Fig 59 The dimensions of the cast-iron ribs, High Level Bridge, Newcastle

IV High Level Bridge, Newcastle

The following calculations are developed from Captain R. M. Laffans' (Royal Engineers) report to the Commissioners of Railways dated 11 August 1849. The dimensions of each of the 125ft span cast-iron arch ribs are shown in Fig 59. The rise of the arch is 17ft 6in and the wrought-iron tie bars at deck level are 7in x 1.0in. There are four ties at the outer arches and eight at the inner arches. The total area of ties is thus:

$$= \quad 2 \times 8 \times 7 \times 1 + 2 \times 4 \times 7 \times 1$$
$$= \quad 168 \text{in}^2 \, (0.108 \times 10^6 \text{mm}^2)$$

The total area of cast iron at the crown of the arch is

=	4 x 12 x 2	=	96
	4 x 12 x 3	=	144
	2 x 3 x 36	=	216
	2 x 2 x 38	=	152

$$608 \text{in}^2 \, (0.392 \times 10^6 \text{mm}^2)$$

This ignores any increase in area due to the mouldings. The total uniformly distributed load arising from the weight of the structure was estimated to be 700 tons. The loads from trains, vehicles and pedestrians were estimated as below, resulting in a total uniformly distributed load on the 125ft (38.5m) span of 1,220 tons (12,200kN).

Weight of structure	=	700
Three 100 ton trains	=	300
Vehicles and pedestrians	=	220
Total	=	1,220 tons (12,200kN)

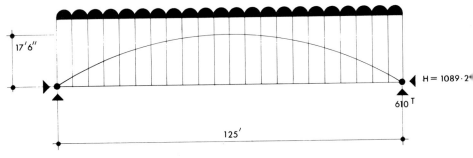

Fig 60 The total load for a 125ft (38m) span arch rib is 1,220 tons

The horizontal thrust H is given by (Fig 60):

$$H = \frac{1220 \times 125}{8 \times 17.5}$$
$$= 1089.29 \text{ tons } (10892.9\text{kN})$$

$$\text{Tension in wrought-iron ties} = \frac{1089.29}{168}$$
$$= 6.48 \text{ tons/in}^2 \ (100.2\text{N/mm}^2)$$

Compression in cast-iron arch rib at crown

$$= \frac{1089.29}{608}$$
$$= 1.79 \text{ tons/in}^2 \ (27.7\text{N/mm}^2)$$

Thus the compressive stress in the arch rib is low, a sensible precaution, as there was no means of calculating the buckling load for curved members in 1850.

228

BIBLIOGRAPHY

The definitive works on the lives of George and Robert Stephenson are those of Samuel Smiles and L. T. C. Rolt. To celebrate the 150th anniversary of the opening of the Liverpool & Manchester Railway in 1980, Hunter Davies has written a lively account of the remarkable life of George Stephenson which includes a useful 'George Stephenson Tour'. The anonymous 'A study of an alleged slight' includes a concise survey of George Stephenson's contribution to the development of railways.

For a general background to the Industrial Revolution and the development of coal mining and transportation systems, reference should be made to Buchanan, Cossons, Dyos and Aldcroft, Morgan, and Singer *et al.*

The most significant of Robert Stephenson's civil engineering works, the Britannia and Conwy tubular bridges are described by Drysdale Dempsey and Fairbairn. In particular, Fairbairn's account of the evolution of the tubular form, the comprehensive series of tests and calculations makes fascinating reading.

Anon. 'A study of an alleged slight' (typescript held at the Institution of Civil Engineers, Great George Street, London)

Bailey, M. R. *Robert Stephenson & Co. 1823–1829* (presented to the Newcomen Society, Science Museum, London, April 1979)

Beckett, D. *Brunel's Britain* (David & Charles, 1980)

Betjeman, J. *London's Historic Railway Stations* (John Murray, 1981)

British Rail, Eastern Region. *The Stockton and Darlington Railway* (published by the Public Relations Officer, 12/74)

British Rail, London Midland Region in association with Avon–Anglia Publications. *Rocket 150, 150th Anniversary of the Liverpool and Manchester Railway 1830–1980* (Official handbook, 1980)

Bruce, G. B. 'Description of the Royal Border Bridge over the River Tweed on the York, Newcastle and Berwick Railway' (proceedings of the Institution of Civil Engineers, February 1851 (219–244))

Brunel, I. *The Life of Isambard Kingdom Brunel, Civil Engineer (1870)* (David & Charles Reprint, 1971)

Buchanan, R. A. *Industrial Archaeology in Britain* (Penguin, 1972)

Carlson, Robert E. *The Liverpool & Manchester Railway Project 1821–1831* (David & Charles, 1969)

Clements, P. *Marc Isambard Brunel* (Longmans, 1970)

Clinker, C. R. *The Leicester and Swannington Railway* (Avon–Anglia Publications and Services, 1977)

Condit, C. W. *American Building Art, The 19th Century* (Oxford University Press, New York, 1960)

Cossons, N. *The BP Book of Industrial Archaeology* (David & Charles, 1975)

Davies, H. *George Stephenson* (Hamlyn Paperbacks, 1980)

Donaghy, Thomas J. *Liverpool & Manchester Railway Operations 1831–1845* (David & Charles, 1972)

Drysdale Dempsey, G. *The Locomotive Engine circa 1850, a rudimentary treatise* (first published 1857, Kingsmead Reprints, 1970)

——*Tubular Bridges circa 1850, a rudimentary treatise* (first published 1864, Kingsmead Reprints 1970)

Duffy, M. C. 'George Stephenson and the Introduction of Rolled Railway Rail', *Journal of Mechanical Working Technology* 5 (1981), 309–42 (Elsevier, 1981)

——'Technomorphology and the Stephenson Traction System' (presented to the Newcomen Society, Science Museum London, December 1982)

Dyos, H. J. and Aldcroft, D. H. *British Transport — An Economic Survey from the Seventeenth Century to the Twentieth* (Pelican, 1974)

Fairbairn, W. *An Account of the Construction of the Britannia and Conway Tubular Bridges* (John Weale and Longman, Brown, Green and Longmans, London, 1849)

Ferneyhough, F. *Liverpool and Manchester Railway 1830–1980* (Book Club Associates, London, 1980)

Fitzgerald, R. S. *Liverpool Road Station Manchester* (Manchester University Press in association with the Royal Commission on Historical Monuments and the Greater Manchester Council, 1980)

Hadfield, C. and Skempton, A. W. *William Jessop, Engineer* (David & Charles, 1979)

Husband, H. C. and R. W. 'Reconstruction of the Britannia Bridge, Part i: Design, Part ii: Construction' (Paper 7704, Proceedings of the Institution of Civil Engineers, Part i: vol 58, February 1975 (25–66))

Jeafferson, J. C. (with Pole, W.) *The Life of Robert Stephenson* (London, Longman, Roberts & Green, 1864)

Jenkins, K. *Montreal, Island City of the St Lawrence* (Doubleday, 1966)

Laffen, B. N. 'Notes upon the High Level Bridge at Newcastle' (Reports of the Commissioners of Railways for the year 1849, Appendix No 50 (83–85))

Law, R. J. *The Steam Engine* (Science Museum) (Her Majesty's Stationery Office, 1977)

Marshall, J. *The Guinness Book of Rail Facts and Figures* (second edition, Guinness Superlatives Ltd, 1975)

Mika, N. and H. *Railways of Canada, A Pictorial History,* (McGraw-Hill Ryerson, 1972)

Morgan, B. *Railways Civil Engineering* (Arrow, 1973)

Pontydd Menai/The Menai Bridges (Welsh Arts Council and Gwynedd Archives Service, 1980)

Rennison, R. W. 'The High Level Bridge, Newcastle: Its Evolution, Design and Construction' (Transactions of the Newcomen Society, Vol 52, 1980–1)

Rolt, L. T. C. *George & Robert Stephenson, The Railway Revolution* (Pelican, 1978)

Roscoe, T. *The London & Birmingham Railway* (Charles Tilt, London, 1833)

Serpell, Sir David. 'The Review of Railway Finances and supplementary volume' (Her Majesty's Stationery Office, 1983)

Sibly, P. 'The Prediction of Structural Failures' (PhD thesis, University of London, Department of Civil Engineering, University College London, 1977)

Singer *et al.* *A History of technology, volume iv, The Industrial Revolution* (c1750 to c1850) (The Clarenden Press, 1975)

Skeat, W. O. *George Stephenson, The Engineer and his Letters* (The Institution of Mechanical Engineers, 1973)

Smiles, S. *Lives of the Engineers, The Locomotive, George & Robert Stephenson* (new & revised edition) (Murray, 1877)

——*Lives of the Engineers*, vol 3 (John Murray 1862, David & Charles reprint, 1968)

Sutherland, R. J. M. 'Thomas Tredgold (1788–1829): Some aspects of his work, part 3 (Transactions of the Newcomen Society, Vol 51, 1979–80)

Swinburne, H. 'Account of the Sea-Walls at Penmaen Mawr, on the line of the Chester and Holyhead Railway' (proceedings of the Institution of Civil Engineers, paper No 806, March 1851)

Sylvester, C. *Report on Rail–Roads and Locomotive Engines 1825* (E. & W. Books (Publishers) Ltd, 1970, a facsimile of the 1825 edition)

van Riemsdijk, J. T. 'The Hero as Engineer' (The George Stephenson Bicentenary Lecture, proceedings of the Institution of Mechanical Engineers, vol 195, no 28, 1981)

Wales Tourist Board (Bwrdd Croeso Cymru). *A Glimpse of the Past* (1981)

Westcott G. F. *The British Railway Locomotive 1803–1853* (Science Museum) (Her Majesty's Stationery Office, 1972)

ACKNOWLEDGEMENTS

Following their immeasurable contribution to *Brunel's Britain*, Frances Gibson-Smith and Malcolm Kaye have again prepared the photographs and illustrations which are so essential to a book of this nature. Their continuing support is greatly appreciated. My secretary, Inez Mason, has conquered my left-handed scrawl to produce the typed text with great rapidity and this has been a spur to meet a deadline, which can so easily slip back. Information supplied by the following is acknowledged:

R. Travers Morgan & Partners, Consulting Engineers on the North Wales Coast Road (A55). Husband & Co, Consulting Engineers and Architects on the reconstruction of the Britannia Bridge. The Science Museum Library for access to Robert Stephenson's letters. Professor Alistair Walker, University of Surrey, for access to P. G. Silby's stimulating thesis on the prediction of structural failures which forms the background to Chapter 5, together with the assistance of Paul Gardiner. The Canadian High Commission Reference Library for information on the Victoria Bridge, Montreal. The Science Museum Photographic Section. The National Portrait Gallery. The National Coal Board for data on mining. Professor G. S. Emmerson for kindly obtaining photographs of the Victoria Bridge, Montreal. The libraries of the Institution of Civil Engineers and the Institution of Mechanical Engineers.

In bringing this book to completion, there were many hours of quiet desperation and the constant encouragement of Paul and Margaret Marsh, Stephen and Pam Griffiths, Rita and Ralph Williamson, Roger Bishop and Mark Lister will not be forgotten.

Finally, I would like to express my appreciation of the support of colleagues at Sir Frederick Snow & Partners and the helpful guidance of Anthony Lambert in editorial matters.

INDEX

A5 trunk road, 77, 92
Aldbury, 89
Aldcroft, D. H., 77
Alderson, Edward, 44
Alexandria & Cairo Railway, 177
Alton Grange, 98
Atmospheric railway system, 191

Bagworth incline, 67
Bailey, M. R., 63, 177
Baltimore & Ohio Railway, 177
Bank Top Station, 38
Beamish North of England Open
    Air Museum, 38, 40, 212
Beckett, D., 75, 142, 191
Betts, E. L., 178
Birkinshaw, John, 41
Birmingham International Station,
    107
Black Callerton, 27
Black Diamond, locomotive, 38
Blackett, Christopher, 17, 19
Blenkinsop, John, 17, 24
Blisworth canal tunnel, 78
Blisworth cutting, 81, 92, 94, 95
Blucher, locomotive, 22, 24
Bogotá, Colombia, 176
Booth, Henry, 54, 177
Boulton, Matthew, 15
Bourne, J. C., 85, 89, 96, 98, 99
Bramah, Joseph, 146
Brassey, Thomas, 79, 178
Britannia Tubular Bridge, 26;
    development of tubular form,
    132; Fairbairn's tests, 135;
    dimensions of tubes, 138;
    construction sequence, 139;
    thermal movement, 141; floating
    the tubes, 145; lifting the tubes,
    146; the fire, 147; technical
    assessment, 218, 226
Brooke, David, 83
Bruce, George Barclay, 166
Brunel, Isambard Kingdom, 5, 24,
    26, 118, 120, 129, 131, 142, 186,
    189, 191, 193
Brunel, Marc Isambard 5, 23, 26,
    184
Brusselton incline, 38
Burrell, John and Issac, 40
Bury, Edward, 102

Canterbury & Whitstable
    Railway, 25, 65, 66
Carol Green Tunnel, 81, 100
Carr, Mabel, 27, 29
Cartegena, Colombia, 17, 176
Carus, Dr C. G., 109
Catch me who can, locomotive, 17,
    18, 24
Chapman, William, 49
Chat Moss bog, 52
Chester & Holyhead Railway,
    Telford's routes, 108;
    Stephenson's route, 111; stations,
    111; sea walls, 115; A55 coast
    road, 115, 119
Clanny, W. R., 33
Clements, P., 184
Clinker, C. R., 67, 69
Coal mining, 11-13
Cock Inn, Stony Stratford, 85
Cogged rail, 21
Coleman, Terry, 83
Colombian Mining Association, 64,
    175

Comet, locomotive, 69
Condit, C. W., 179
Conwy Tubular Bridge, 25;
  development of tubular form,
  132; Fairbairn's tests, 135;
  dimensions of tubes, 138;
  construction sequence, 139;
  floating and raising the tubes,
  142; technical assessment, 218-26
Curzon Street Station,
  Birmingham, 100, 101

Damietta, Egypt, 177
Darby, Abraham I, 120
Darby, Abraham II, 120
Darby, Abraham III, 121
Davy, Sir Humphrey, 33, 34
Dee Bridge collapse, properties of
  cast iron, 121; Hodgkinson
  formula, 121; wrought iron, 121,
  122; the trussed girder, 123;
  construction of bridge, 125;
  collapse and factors contributing,
  126-8; enquiry, 129; Brunel's
  comments, 129; technical
  assessment, 216-18
Delaware & Hudson Canal Co, 176
Dempsey, G. Drysdale, 111, 125,
  141
Denbigh Hall, 91, 92, 102
Dewley Burn, 27
Dial Cottage, 186, 211
Diligence, locomotive, 38
Dixon, John, 52, 65
Dr Bruce's School, 186
Dudley Castle, 23
Duffy, M. C., 57
Dyos, H. J., 77

Edinburgh University, 63
Etherley incline, 38
Euston Station, 104, 105

Fairbairn, William, 50, 51, 121,
  134, 138, 218
Ferneyhough, F., 44
Fire-damp, 32, 33

Fitzgerald, R. S., 49, 51
Florence & Leghorn Railway, 130
Forth Street, Newcastle, 63

Gaunless Bridge, 38, 40, 42, 43
Glamorganshire canal, 17
Glenfield Tunnel, 67
Gooch, Daniel, 190
Grand Allies, 9
Grand Junction Canal, 77, 78
Grand Junction Railway, 25, 79, 80
Grand Trunk Railway, 178, 179
Gray, T., 194, 196
Great Eastern, steamship, 142
Great Hall, Euston Station, 105
Great Western Railway, 88, 189
Gregory, Ellen, 25, 29, 62

Hadfield, C., 78
Hampstead Road Bridge, 85, 86
Hardwick, Philip, 104
Hardwick, Philip C., 105
Hawkes, Crawshay & Co , 17
Hawkins, G., 144, 145, 146
Hedley, William, 19, 24
Hemel Hempstead, 89
Henderson, Frances, 24, 29
Hetton colliery, 34
High Level Bridge, Newcastle, 25,
  26; early Tyne bridges, 153;
  structural form, 155;
  foundations, 156; piers, 159;
  deck structure, 159
Hindmarsh, Elizabeth, 24, 31
Hodge, James, 178
Hodgkinson, Eaton, 50, 51, 121
Hodgkinson's formula, 121
Holy Trinity Church, Chesterfield,
  26, 60, 213
Hope, locomotive, 38
Horse runs, 90
Howick, Lord, 192
Hudson, George, 70, 71
Husband & Co, 148
Husband, H. C. & R. W., 148
Hutchinson, F. W., 147

Institution of Civil Engineers, 24, 26, 60, 62, 74, 202
Institution of Mechanical Engineers, 24, 26, 62, 74, 201
Invicta, locomotive, 65
Ironbridge, 122
Ironbridge Gorge Museum, 121
Irwell, River, 49, 52

James, William, 44, 65
Jeafferson, J. C., 100, 182
Jenkins, K., 178
Jessop, William, 62, 77
Jolly's Close, 27, 31

Kensal Green cemetery, 88
Kensal Green Tunnel, 81
Killingworth, 31
Killingworth colliery, 21
Kilsby Tunnel, 81, 98, 99, 100

La Guayra, Venezuela, 175
Laffan, R. M. 156
Lake Miosen, 177
Lancashire Witch, locomotive, 54
Lardner, Dr Dionysius, 22
Leicester & Swannington Railway, 25, 65-9
Leighton Buzzard, 90
Leopold I, King of Belgium, 177
Liddell, H. T., 22
Liddell, Sir Thomas (Lord Ravensworth), 21
Linslade Tunnel, 81, 90
Literary and Philosophical Institute, Newcastle, 63, 185
Liverpool & Manchester Railway, 22, 25; early proposals, 44; surveys, 44; George Stephenson's cross-examination, 44; the Rennies's and Vignoles's involvement, 45; route and gradients, 45-7; the track, 45; civil engineering works, 48-52; Chat Moss bog, 52; locomotive competition, 53; Rainhill trials, 54; the *Rocket*, 54, 55; the *Planet*, 54, 56; Fanny Kemble, 57, 58
Liverpool Road Station, Manchester, 49
Livingstone, Dr David, 74, 76
Llanfairpwll, 111, 208
Locke, Joseph, 79
Locomotion, 38, 39, 212
Locomotive and track development, 34, 35
London & Birmingham Railway, estimate, 71; survey, 80; divisions, 81; navvies, 83; contractors and contracts, 84; the route, 85; gradients, 85; Euston cutting, 86; Primrose Hill Tunnel, 87; Kensal Green, 88; Watford Tunnel, 89; Tring cutting, 89; Linslade Tunnel, 90; Denbigh Hall Bridge, 92; Wolverton embankment and viaduct, 92; Blisworth/Roade cutting, 92-5; Kilsby Tunnel 81, 98, 99, 100; Curzon Street, 100; Euston portico, 105; Great Hall, 105
Long Benton, 63
Longridge, Michael, 63
Losh, William, 34, 40

M1 Motorway, 77
Magdalena, River, 176
Menai Strait, 132
Menai Suspension Bridge, 133
Methane gas, 33
Mexican Mining Association, 63
Middleton collieries, 17
Mid Hill, 27
Montrose, 31
Morgan, B., 80
Murdock, William, 16, 24
Murray, Matthew, 17
Mylne, Robert, 153

Nasmyth, William, 158, 167
National Railway Museum, York, 40, 67, 213
Navvies, 83, 84

New Orleans Railway, 190
Newburn, 27
Newcastle & Berwick Railway, 25
Newcastle & Darlington Junction
    Railway, 70
Newcomen, Thomas, 13-15, 23
Niagara Falls Suspension Bridge,
    179
Northchurch Tunnel, 81, 89
North Road Station, Darlington, 38
North Star, locomotive, 190
North Western Museum of Science
    & Technology, 52

Overton, George, 35, 36

Pease, Edward, 35, 63, 176
Penydarren ironworks, 17
Penmaenmawr sea walls, 114
Penmaenbach headland, 114
Percy Street, Newcastle, 63
Peto, Samuel Morton, 82
Planet, locomotive, 22
Pontop & South Shields Railway, 70
Primrose Hill Tunnel, 81

Rack locomotive, 17, 19
Rainhill Bridge, 49
Ravensworth, Lord, 22
Regent's Canal Bridge, 86, 87
Rennie, George, 44
Rennie, John, 44
Rennison, R. W., 153
Richardson, Thomas, 63
Riemsdijk, J. T. van, 5
Robert Stephenson & Co, 38, 63,
    177
Rocket, locomotive, 25
Roebling, J. A., 179
Rolt, L. T. C., 5, 22, 33, 34, 41, 60,
    65, 70, 75, 80, 85, 89, 131, 145,
    177, 188
Roscoe, T., 71
Ross, Alexander, 178
Round House, Chalk Farm, 74,
    102, 103, 104, 105, 202
Royal Albert Bridge, Saltash, 131

Royal Border Bridge, Berwick upon
    Tweed, 26; foundations, 166;
    piers, 169; arches, 170
Royal Society, 23, 26, 34, 74
Russell, John Scott, 74, 75

Safety Lamp, 33, 34
St Lawrence River, 178
Samuda, Jacob and Joseph, 191
Sanderson, Fanny, 25, 65
Sankey Viaduct, 50
Savery, Thomas, 13, 23
Science Museum, London, 201
Seguin, Marc, 54
Serpell Report, 194
Sibley, P., 125, 130
Singer *et al*, 33, 121
Skempton, A. W., 78
Skew arch bridge, 48-50
Smeaton, John, 15, 23, 62
Smeatonian Society, 62
Smiles, Samuel, 8, 29, 59, 71, 84,
    176, 186, 192
Society of Civil Engineers, 62
Spiral method of arch construction,
    49
Spur wheel, 20, 21
Stanhope & Tyne Railway, 70, 71
Steam, development of steam
    engines, 13-22
Stephenson, George, 5, 24, 26, 29;
    early life, 27; family tree, 29;
    work in pits, 27-32; safety lamp,
    33, 34; track development, 34,
    35; Stockton & Darlington
    Railway, 35-43; Liverpool &
    Manchester Railway, 44-58; life
    at Tapton House, 59; death, 62;
    education, 184
Stephenson, Robert, 5, 26, 29;
    education, 29, 186; locomotive
    works, 63; Canterbury &
    Whitstable Railway, 65;
    Leicester & Swannington
    Railway, 65; Stanhope & Tyne
    Railway, 70-1; London &
    Birmingham Railway, 71, 77-107;

honours, 74, 76; death, 76;
Chester & Holyhead Railway,
108-19; Dee Bridge, 120-30;
Britannia and Conwy bridges,
131-51; Tyne and Tweed bridges,
153-73; work overseas, 175-83
Stockton & Darlington Railway, 24,
25, 35-43
Stockton Steam Boat Company, 63
Stow Hill Tunnel, 81
Sutherland, R. J. M., 51
Sutton incline, 45
Swannington incline, 67
Swinburne, H., 114
Sylvester, Charles, 35

Tapton House, Chesterfield, 59,
213
Telford, Thomas, 62, 76, 77, 108,
109, 132, 151
Thomas, John, 58
Throckley Bridge, 27
Titania, yacht, 75
Travers Morgan & Partners, R., 115
Tredgold, Thomas, 51
Trevithick, Richard, 16, 17, 24, 176
Tring cutting, 81, 89

Trussed cast-iron girders, 123

Victoria Tubular Bridge, Montreal,
26, 131
Vignoles, Charles Blacker, 45, 52,
123

Water Street Bridge, 50-2
Watford Gap, 77
Watford Tunnel, 81, 89
Watt, James, 15, 23, 24
West Moor colliery, 32
Westminster Abbey, 76
Whiston incline, 45
Whitby, 25
Wilkinson, John, 15, 24
Willington Quay, 31, 63
Wolverton embankment, 81, 92
Wolverton Viaduct, 92, 93
Wood, Nicholas, 63
Wylam, 24, 27
Wylam colliery, 17, 19, 27
Wylam Dilly, locomotive, 19
Wylam plateway, 19

York & North Midland Railway, 70